By the Same Author

Note Found in a Bottle
A Woman's Life
Treetops
Elizabeth Cole
Doctors and Women
Home Before Dark
The Cage
Handsome Man
Looking for Work

AS GOOD
AS I COULD BE

A Memoir
of Raising Wonderful Children
in Difficult Times

SUSAN CHEEVER

SIMON & SCHUSTER

NEW YORK   LONDON   TORONTO   SYDNEY   SINGAPORE

Simon & Schuster
Rockefeller Center
1230 Avenue of the Americas
New York, NY 10020

10   9   8   7   6   5   4   3   2   1

Library of Congress Cataloging-in-Publication Data

Cheever, Susan.
  As good as I could be : a memoir about raising
wonderful children in difficult times / Susan Cheever.
      p.   cm.
    1. Mothers—Psychology.   2. Mother and child.
3. Parenting.   4. Child rearing.   I. Title.
HQ759.C515 2001
306.874'3—dc21   2001020068

ISBN 0-684-86341-3

For my beloved children,
and for all the wonderful adults
who have helped me raise them.
Thank you.

CONTENTS

PART ONE

Real Me • 15

The Birth of a Child • 18

The Birth of a Parent • 26

Might Makes Right? • 34

Teacher Versus Parent • 42

Stepmother • 45

Please Don't Go! • 52

Tantrums • 58

Divorce • 66

It's Not the Divorce That Hurts • 73

Children and Therapy • 79

School • 84

Inventing Adolescence • 92

Baby-sitters • 99

My Daughter Searches for God • 107

PART TWO

Rabbit in the Snow • 115

Comforts • 119

Does Money Help? • 124

Clothes • 130

The Pedagogy of Parenting: How Do Children Learn? • 134

The Ethics of Parenting • 142

Pets • 147

Teenagers: Why We Hate Them. Why They Hate Us. • 154

Avoiding the Broccoli Battles • 159

Eating Disorders • 162

Children and Alcohol • 168

How Love Works • 174

Believe • 178

Epilogue • 188

Acknowledgments • 190

As Good
as I Could Be

The value of marriage is not that adults produce children,
but that children produce adults.

—PETER DE VRIES

PART ONE

PART ONE

REAL ME

WHEN MY DAUGHTER WAS BORN eighteen years ago, my brother Fred and his wife sent her a stuffed brown bear with a white nose and tummy and a manufacturer's name tag which told us its name was "Snuffles." Snuffles joined the piles of plush bears, dogs, cats, frogs, and clowns in her room; she was my first child and my parents' first grand-daughter, two facts which seemed to provoke stuffed animal buying or-gies on the part of otherwise sensible people. But slowly, as she grew and learned to grab, cuddle, and express preferences, she gravitated to-ward Snuffles. As soon as she could gesture, she let us know that Snuf-fles needed to be in her crib at night. She began regularly falling asleep with her tiny hands nestling in the bear's soft fur. Like all first-time mothers, I had read every baby book from Dr. Spock and Penelope Leach to Margaret Mahler, and I knew that the bear was my daughter's transitional object. I was proud of everything she did, and settling on such an appealing transitional object seemed further evidence of her exceptional intelligence.

Of course she didn't call the bear Snuffles. She was ten months old and innocent of the silly names provided by manufacturers for their products. She didn't even realize it was a bear. She thought it was a male cat and she called it Meow, which she shortened to Me. Me the bear became her most beloved thing, the center of her secure world.

"Where's my Me?" she would ask, in her sweet little voice. "Where's Me?"

What the baby books forgot to mention was the devastating effect of too much love. By the time my daughter was two years old, Me was worn and tattered from being caressed, his once gleaming fur had been fondled to a dull, tufted fabric, his button eyes were missing, and his smile kissed away. After a citywide hunt, I located another Me—a new Snuffles—and brought him home triumphantly. My daughter was less than pleased. She added the new bear to her menagerie and continued to sleep with the worn-out old one, amending his name to "Real Me" to distinguish him from the impostor.

By the time my daughter turned three, Real Me was a sorry sight. As he became more tattered, he seemed to become more necessary— especially after my daughter gave up the bottle which had lulled her to sleep. She couldn't even think about bedtime until Real Me was ensconced on her pillow. When we traveled, Real Me was the first thing I packed. As he crumbled, my anxieties soared. What if he was lost? What if he just came apart at the seams one day after a particularly energetic hug? I was convinced that if that happened my daughter would never sleep again. When I slept, I sometimes had nightmares about Real Me. In my dreams he disappeared or disintegrated as I watched helplessly. My psychiatrist asked if I thought my marriage was disintegrating.

One day, shopping in a downtown department store, the escalator took me past the toy department. There, displayed as if he was meant for me to see, was another new Snuffles. This time, I had him wrapped in plain brown paper. That night while my little girl slept, I massacred this new Snuffles with a pair of scissors, reducing him to parts—eyes, nose, ears, and swatches of fur. I crept into her bedroom and stealthily took Real Me from her pillow. With an ear cocked toward the room where she innocently dreamed, I hastily sewed on one new plush leg.

I had a restless night. Had I tampered with the thing my daughter cared about the most, and ruined it forever? Had I failed to respect her feelings for the one object in the household which belonged to her and her alone? Would she notice and be horrified? The next morning I held my breath. She didn't comment. That night at bedtime, I watched terrified as she stroked the new leg in her sleepy ritual. "Mmmm, soft," she said. After that, every few weeks, I replaced a tiny part of Real Me with a part from the new Snuffles. I have continued to replace parts of Real Me with dozens of parts from new Snuffleses I have bought over the years. After a few years, my daughter realized what was happening, but by then my replacement rituals had become as much a part of Real Me as the bear himself, and she accepted the fact that he was a patchwork of old and new.

Real Me sits on my computer as I write this, one-eyed and tattered, his tail all but worn off. It's been a few years since I have replaced a part. As he is fondled less, he wears better. My daughter is with her father this weekend (our marriage *was* disintegrating). These days Real Me sleeps at the end of her bed in a pile of quilts. She doesn't notice him much, and when she leaves she doesn't take him with her. Her security comes from other things now. I still keep him though: he's a memento of that time long ago when my teenager was a baby, and a proof that although too much love can destroy, it can also repair and mend.

THE BIRTH
OF A CHILD

I WAS THIRTY-EIGHT when I had my first child, my precious daughter. It was late on a Monday night, the day after Easter in April of 1982. The British were preparing to invade the Falklands, and John Updike and Sylvia Plath had just won the Pulitzer Prize. I had been married less than a year. My father was dying of cancer. None of that mattered at all. The birth of my daughter divided my life into a one-dimensional "before" and a rich, deep, and human "after."

As the doctor performed a C-section and my husband held my hand, I seemed to drift away from the scene in the operating room. When they were all finished, I would have a baby. I congratulated myself on the arrangements I had made in advance. I had a baby-nurse and a nanny. The nanny had already been cleaning our apartment for months so that I could get to know her. We had picked out a pediatrician, after interviewing three who had been recommended by friends. We had chosen the one with the organized office and the wallpaper patterned with garden trellises. We had gone down to Orchard Street in the car and loaded up with a crib, a changing table, and a bassinet. We had a diaper pail and a complete layette.

A series of baby showers had provided us with stuffed bears, receiving blankets, and half a dozen mobiles. The announcements were ready for the printer. We knew the baby's name. She would be Liley—

my father's mother's maiden name. I was of the opinion that I probably wouldn't like the baby at first, and so I had been sure to protect myself against her intrusion into my life. I was a writer, a woman, a lover, and a friend. I just couldn't see myself as a mother.

In the moment that I held my baby daughter in my arms, in that operating room at New York Hospital, I changed so fast that I felt dizzy. I instantly loved her and wanted to protect her. Loving her became the focus of my existence, and somehow that love included all other mothers and all other children and the whole human family, a phrase which in the past would have made me snort with derision. To my surprise, after almost forty years, I became vulnerable. With each moment, with each tiny sound or gesture, my baby girl provoked more love and more and more until I was awash in this delicious and unfamiliar feeling.

My senses seemed awakened for the first time—as if all my previous feelings, all the perfumes and delights of my life, had happened to someone in a movie. The feel of my baby's skin was like a rose petal, like an angel's wing, there were no words to describe the way it felt to me. The smells of her little body, the soft warmth at the top of her head, and the way her little perfect hands smelled when she brushed my face, made me feel as if I had never had a nose before.

The physical deliciousness of my baby was nothing compared to what I felt inside. I could actually feel my heart expanding and blossoming beneath my skin. All the feelings I had before seemed silly and petty. What had I known of love? It wasn't even as if the feelings that I had before were some kind of practice for the feelings I had for my daughter—they were of another magnitude, as if I had been living by starlight and had suddenly walked into the sun. My heart thawed in an instant. Feelings I didn't know existed poured—and it literally felt as if they were pouring out of me—toward my tiny daughter. I thought I was going to melt.

All the things they say about love, the kind of love they write songs about, suddenly seemed insignificant. Nothing that a man or any adult could do—not making a million dollars or bringing home roses or cooking a great meal—could make me feel the way my baby's tiniest gesture or welcoming smile could make me feel. She was infinitely fascinating. Everyone else was boring. When I held her I could feel my center of gravity shift over until it was as if I was floating, floating with my baby on a cloud beyond anyone else's reach. My whole life shifted with her smile, and darkened with her crying.

I had spent my life trying to connect and find meaning. I had traveled, I had loved many men, I had read and studied and worshiped. In the moment of my daughter's birth I found everything I had been searching for in all those ways over all those years. It was as if my soul opened out to embrace her—and in opening out my soul made itself known to me. This rush of feeling became like a scent that pervaded everything I did, and everything I remembered. As my baby grew, my love grew right along with her. That love gave me energy and sharp eyes and the ability to get along without sleep. Most of all it gave me a person to be—a mother.

The birth of a child is also the birth of a parent. As I settled down to raise my daughter, I began to learn the most important lessons of my life. With her, and later with my son, who was born seven years later, I was gently forced to learn about the special kind of intimacy which exists between parents and children. Before Liley was born, I was a child myself. After she was born, I began the long process of becoming an adult—a process which interested me only because I wanted to be a good mother for her. I knew, and this was the first true thing, that only an adult could take care of a child. I was forced to understand the special kind of authority which parents have over their children.

One of the little known facts about pregnancy is that it actually lasts from two to five years. It's a progression, from the conception of an embryo to the fully developed, walking, talking child. Childbirth is just one point on the continuum. For months and months after Liley's birth, it felt to me as if my daughter and I were still joined in our bodies as well as in our souls. Any separation was indescribably painful. When I was with her, I was whole—my two parts were reunited. When I was on the other side of town, I was torn in two. Even when I thought she was safe, and I was very anxious about her safety, missing her still felt like a visceral tearing, like an internal amputation.

Love raised a lot of questions. The other side of love isn't hate, I don't think. It's being paralyzed. It's a flash of helpless anger which grabs you up for one murderous minute and then drops you, panting, back into ordinary life. When I could comfort my daughter by nursing her or singing to her or staying up with her all night, gently moving her mobiles and cooing to her, I was in ecstacy. I felt as if every cell in my body was rejoicing. When she cried out in pain, long shrieky cries, and nothing I could do made any difference, I wanted to flee; I wanted to die.

She was a sleeper, my little girl, but late in the afternoon her whole world seemed to tilt toward misery. She would murmur unhappily as some imbalance in her body took hold, and then give way to crying. All my comforting, my rocking and singing and playing loud music and splashing in the kitchen sink, had no effect. She didn't want to eat. She didn't want to play. She pushed away the bottle and hurled the pacifier on the floor.

Being born is a painful thing. Babies' neurological and digestive systems aren't entirely developed. As a result, babies cry a lot. When my baby cried, every nerve in my body sang with anxiety. I was happy to stay up all night, to sing and dance for hours, to walk the streets of New York with the baby clutched next to me in the front pack. When I couldn't calm her, though, my nerves vibrated and jittered panic; I felt as if I was going to jump out of my skin. Her crying elicited a level of distress and agitation in me that I have rarely known before or since.

No one who hasn't heard their own baby cry ceaselessly can know what this is like. I would have done anything to quiet her. I learned to hand her to the baby-sitter or my husband and leave the room, take ten deep breaths and then come back. Thank God for the baby-sitter. Thank God for the patience that comes with age. I knew that my baby hadn't chosen to be born. I knew that her existence was my responsibility, and that somehow, some way—and on many days this seemed impossible—I would have to learn to take care of her.

WHAT MADE my predicament worse was that I had come to believe one of the great American myths—the myth of the natural mother. I grew up thinking that parenting in general and mothering in particular was something a woman could just do without preparation, like having a period or enjoying sex, or bearing a child in the first place. I thought that a good woman would naturally know how to diaper a baby, hold a baby, bathe a baby, comfort a baby, and breast-feed a baby. The truth is that taking care of a baby is not easy, and that doing it well is a learned skill just like any other. In the few days I spent in the hospital there were lessons in bathing the baby and holding the baby, but none of us paid much attention. We all thought that a "good mother" didn't need lessons. We all had the mistaken impression that if we loved our babies we would somehow know how to take care of them.

I had imagined childbirth as a rosy experience conducted to the score of a soprano singing "Amazing Grace," and I had imagined that my baby would be put to my breast and suck hungrily. I was proud that I didn't have any hang-ups about my body. I knew it well; I liked it fine. I assumed this would make breast-feeding a cinch. My precious infant daughter, however, did not seem to have gotten the message. She nuzzled and hummed, but when my breast happened into her mouth and she happened to suck for a second or two she seemed to lose interest.

As hours and then days went by and my daughter failed to latch on to my breast, my anxiety soared. She needed to eat. She needed milk desperately. Yet somehow the system—a system which I imagined was already in place—wasn't working. I tried pumping milk from my breasts and feeding it to her in a bottle. That worked, but of course it diminished the likelihood of her sucking at my breasts. I felt like a complete failure. I had no idea how to take care of my baby—the one being in the world I had ever really wanted to care for. I couldn't even feed her correctly.

The doctors shrugged and suggested that formula would make our lives easier. My husband wasn't too concerned either. Formula allowed him to take more part in her care, he pointed out. By the time I called the La Leche League, it was way too late. Within a week, because of Liley's jaundice, the doctor had decreed that I shouldn't breast-feed anyway.

I LIKE TO SAY that it's lucky I didn't start having children when I was in my twenties. I know now that, if there had been time, I would have had ten. Having children is like eating chocolate—the more you have the more you want. After the first pleasure-stunned months of life with Liley, even after the difficulties of loving so passionately had emerged, I wanted another child. I didn't know how I could have gotten through life in general, and the death of my father in particular, without my brothers. I love my brothers and they often save my life in dozens of ways. The real reason that I wanted another child, though, was selfish. Having a child was so delicious, so amazing, such a complete awakening of my sleeping soul, that I wanted more. For six years, though, I resigned myself to being the mother of a single girl, and I was content.

Then in 1989 I got pregnant again, at the age of forty-five. My new husband was eager for a child—although he already had two grown daughters. And if I couldn't believe the rush of love that I got with my first baby, I was even more incredulous when it happened all over again. Love is not limited. Love makes love. Falling in love with my baby boy, as I did completely and utterly, in no way diminished my love for my little girl.

My son was born on a Friday night. My husband and I were sitting around thinking about what to eat, inasmuch as someone as pregnant as I was can just sit around. Suddenly I had severe cramps and started to leak water. My water broke with a gush. Ten towels later, I wondered what happened to people with wall-to-wall carpets. I had read about a woman who carried a jar of pickles with her everywhere, so that if her water broke she could drop the jar of pickles to cover her embarrassing condition. I would have had to carry a gallon jug. Then the contractions started. At about dawn I bundled up in my husband's coat and we got in a cab to the hospital. I was filled with a tremendous sense of security and gratitude for the abundance of the universe. I lay in a sunny room at Mount Sinai while the nurse put in a Pitocin drip and an anesthesiologist painlessly slid the needle for the epidural into my spine.

I was expectant and happy instead of being afraid as I had been seven years earlier during the birth of my daughter. My son apparently didn't share my optimism. He didn't want to be born. Contraction after contraction, push after push, he stayed stubbornly away from the birth canal. Morning turned to afternoon. The gynecologist—a wonderful man—might well have done a cesarean section. After all, I was a forty-six-year-old woman. Instead he said, "I think we'll practice the art of *sitzfleisch*," and he sat down on a chair at the end of the bed. We had decided to wait my son out.

We chatted. The gynecologist told me about his mother. We talked about the piano lessons we had as children. The afternoon passed. It was Saturday, but the nurses who had seen me come in wanted to wait for the birth of my son. Now we were all waiting for him. At last my beloved boy started to move. I was wheeled into the operating room, fully conscious, and watched in delight as the doctor pulled him out. Everyone clapped. It was three-thirty-three on the afternoon of November the fourth.

With my son, I succeeded in breast-feeding, but it took hours and days of effort. At first I spent whole afternoons waiting for him to breast-feed. I watched *Oprah*. Feeding time, which happened almost every three hours, was as much about patience as it was about providing. We finally worked out a rhythm between us and breast-feeding him was profoundly satisfying. It also made travel with him very easy. He never cried or got cranky in public. Being able to feed him on demand made it possible for us to go anywhere together, and we did. I fed him on airplanes and in museums and sitting on the grass at the San Francisco Zoo in front of a cage of monkeys with the music of the carousel in the distance.

I know now that mothering isn't natural. I try not to blame myself for not having learned to breast-feed my daughter. Still, when my daughter gets in trouble, when she's needy or when she gets sick, that's the first thing that pops into my mind. She never got those immunities or that psychological benefit of breast-feeding. I know better, but it feels like a failure, even now.

At the same time, it's still hard for me to believe that I've had much to do with creating my children's excellence and their good hearts, much less the adorable way their hair grows or the tiny string of birthmarks on Liley's porcelain back. That was one of the first things I noticed about her. It looked as if someone had splashed her with something pink just at the moment when she left wherever she left to appear in the operating room at New York Hospital.

My life with my children has taken place in New York apartments, and in the streets and parks of a big city. For the last eight years we have lived in a rental apartment with views of brick walls topped by slices of sky. I love the neighborhood of our building and the buildings on our block. It feels like a small town, with a local market and a local Italian restaurant. In the building, the dinnertime smells of other families, the sounds of people living their lives close by, comfort me. When I have left my children alone, neighbors have often looked in on them, and we have returned the favor. My son has had two or three close friends who live in the building. We all feel at home here.

Our furniture is a mixture of chairs inherited from grandparents, a couch purchased in White River Junction, Vermont, twenty years ago, and a few good antiques bought before the children were born. My daughter's room is a mass of books and papers piled on every surface, while my son's room features baskets of toys and shelves of Lego creations and books. There is a wall of bookcases in the living room, another wall in the hall, and a bookcase in my bedroom. Books are piled on almost every available surface. Although I have alphabetized and rearranged my books many times, I often still can't find the book I am looking for.

Our slipcovers are worn, the rugs are woven sisal, and I long ago lost the battle to keep dogs, dirty feet, and stray toys off the furniture. I am a single mother now, since my son's father and I separated amicably six years ago. I am my children's principal financial support, and for the most part, I work at home, on a computer a few feet from my bed. Every family has a different set of circumstances and a different set of problems. Nevertheless, the intensity and complexity of raising our children overwhelms our particular circumstances. Rich or poor, married or single, gay or straight, the task of raising our children is the most exhilarating and extraordinarily difficult task we will ever face.

In order to be a good parent I have had to grow up. The journey has been difficult and punctuated by pratfalls and accidents. Nevertheless, I have learned to be the adult, and this is the hardest part of being a parent. My children have had few of the advantages that are conventionally prescribed for raising children. They have each been through a divorce—and my daughter has lived through the disintegration of two families. We have moved often. Their routines have been disrupted again and again. As a family we have had to deal with serious illness, with financial problems, with alcoholism and eating disorders, with the behavior of divorced fathers, and with the infinitely painful lack of time that dogs every working mother. Yet I have extraordinary children. They are kind and they are smart; they are connected to their friends and family. They do well in school. They delight me and everyone around them. This book is the story of how that happened.

THE BIRTH
OF
A PARENT

MY DAUGHTER SAYS that her first memory is of being awakened by voices raised in anger. She says she got out of the bunk bed and crept from her room toward the living room where her father and I were fighting. I was crying, she says; he was yelling. The ironing board had been set up in the hallway, she remembers, and she hid behind it while she listened to us. The remains of dinner were on the table. We were both standing by the windows near the old blue and white sofa. When she tells me this, my first reaction is self-justification. The best defense, I like to say, is a good *defense*.

Your father never yelled, I want to say. I'm sure I was crying about something else. What about all the good memories? I want to ask. What about everything we did for you before you can even remember? What about the miles of walking you back and forth? The hundreds of diapers and bottles? What about the way I used to rub your back as you drifted off in your crib? What about the pretty dresses and the days we spent pushing you on the swings in the park?

Instead of arguing with her, however, I listen. I desperately want happiness for her. It's hard to accept her saying that in spite of my efforts, her life was never perfect, not even for a moment. I've struggled to understand that she has her own experience of life, and that that experience is not necessarily the one I think she should have had.

"If one can conceive of a fully integrated person, then that person takes responsibility for all feelings and ideas that belong to being alive," writes D. W. Winnicott in *Home Is Where We Start From*. I want my daughter to have happy memories, but I want her to have the freedom to accept the bad things in her experience and in her feelings. Many unattractive and even shameful things happen within families. Pretending that they don't happen only makes them more powerful.

Parenting children is an act of faith. I don't struggle to be a good parent so that my children will remember me as a good parent. It's not nearly that simple or that graphic. I believe, somehow, that the way I behave toward my children has implications beyond memory. I believe that although memory will not reach back into my children's early years, the roots of their character will begin there and those roots will either be nourished or they will wither.

We live in the age of advice. There are nine principles of almost everything, and five simple rules for almost everything else. Nowhere is this more evident than in the avalanche of expertise about bringing up children. In this book I have tried to describe how I have raised my eighteen-year-old daughter and my ten-year-old son. If my experience helps you, or if it makes you feel a little less alone, okay; if it makes you laugh, that's wonderful. There are bookcases of books which tell parents how to do everything from raising a peaceful teenager (male) to raising a thin teenager (female). Much of this advice is flatly contradictory. On any given day a confused parent can be advised:

1. To use punishments and time-outs to control their children's behavior, or to avoid all punishments because they inhibit the development of a conscience.

2. To invest in tutoring, therapy, and "anger management" for toddlers, or to avoid anything which might push toddlers ahead of the natural behavior for their age.

3. To insist on a healthy diet, because children who eat healthy food will want healthy food, or to allow children to choose exactly what they want to eat, because restricting a food makes it attractive.

4. To find a school which nurtures a child and makes him or her happy, or to be sure that the child gets a solid basic education no matter how painful that may be.

5. To supplement a child's education by helping with home-

work—giving the child an audience—and suggesting complementary activities, or to leave the child's education to his or her teacher so that the child can develop independent study habits.

6. To limit television because it keeps a child from developing normal brain synapses, or accept television and video games as part of normal life and the world in which the child must learn to live and grow.

Life would be so much easier if there was someone to tell us how to live it. "Where's the instruction book!" a friend of mine wailed as she held her new baby. Raising children is the hardest, longest, most expensive, most important job any of us will ever have. No wonder we're hungry for advice. But what defines an adult is the ability to take responsibility, and the courage to follow our educated, thoughtful instincts—even when we make mistakes.

In every generation the pendulum swings wildly back and forth between child-raising experts who advocate discipline and structure, and the experts who tell us to listen to our instincts. Currently both methods of raising children—the restrictive and the instinctive—are being aggressively promoted. Our hunger for rules has created a cottage industry and a publishing boom, and made disciplinarian John Rosemond something of a folk hero among parents. At the same time Harvard professor William Pollack's ode to the heart, *Real Boys,* is a solid bestseller.

To make this more complicated, many child-raising experts are psychologists or psychiatrists who have never actually raised children. In most fields, expertise is based on experience, but in raising children it seems to be based on study. When child-raising experts have children, many of them are amazed at the emotional urgency and lack of logic which characterize the process. "During the long hours of our baby's first night when singing, frequent diaper changes, attempts at feeding, and a host of new tricks my wife and I invented on the spur of the moment all failed to end Bess's relentless caterwauling," wrote Professor Howard Markel, author of *The Practical Pediatrician,* in a recent article, "the words that echoed in my mind were, what was I thinking when I wrote that stuff?"

What makes all child-raising advice worthless—whatever we might pay for it—is that each child is different, and every child changes from hour to hour and from week to week. A good education "takes time, it takes patience, it takes the willingness to make exceptions," says educator Ted Sizer. Raising children is one big exception. Every child is unique, every situation is once-in-a-lifetime. Good parenting is a matter of instinct, not policy.

My son, for instance, is sometimes a quiet boy who needs me to walk him up to his classroom and drop by the school at lunchtime with a treat and a hug. At other times he's a grown man, impatient with my fussing, embarrassed by my kisses, and eager to be out in the world on his own. Some nights we do his homework together. Other nights it's between him and his teacher; he needs to do it by himself, and I don't even check his backpack. My daughter in fourth grade was a happy girl whose three best friends were boys. By the fifth grade the school had changed, the friendships had soured, and the class had become the setting for serious misery. In sixth grade the school asked me to have her tutored in mathematics. That wasn't a good idea for her then, but the math tutor she had in tenth grade changed her life.

Sometimes my children need a quick lesson in cause and effect. They need to know that abusing their phone privileges results in withdrawal of phone privileges. However, when my daughter forgot to call one night, and left me wondering where she was—a much more serious offense than any abuse of phone privileges—I saw that her remorse was punishment enough. Children have phases; adults have phases too. Sometimes I can hang out with my children until we all fall asleep on my bed in a happy pile. Other times I am busy or preoccupied. In order to judge each situation well, we need to use our instincts. We need to listen. We need to set aside our own memories and impulses if we can. This is intimacy, and it's scary.

When my son was born, my daughter was seven years old. She had been an adored only child, and although she begged for a baby brother or sister, she came close to changing her mind. She did all the funny things siblings do. She made a sign that said "Baby For Sale: 100 Percent Off" and hung it on his crib. She asked if he could go back to the hospital. Torn between the two people I loved more than anything in the world, I made a smart decision. I remembered that love has to be voluntary; love can't be legislated. I took a chance. I told my daughter that she didn't have to love her baby brother. I told her that she didn't even have to like him. All she had to do was live with him, I said. "Aren't you thrilled to have a little baby brother?" my friends would ask her. "I hate him!" she would say. This made for uncomfortable conversation on the street, but it took the pressure off at home.

In my experience the world is benevolent, and it's often my interference that makes things go wrong. Left to their own devices, my children learned to love each other. It began with my baby son's love for his sister. He worshiped her. It was her voice he responded to, and her presence in a room that made him wriggle and shriek with joy. She could calm him down when no one else could. Her name was one of his first words. She tried to keep hating him, but his total, unconditional adoration was a hard thing to resist.

Eventually, she began to head for his crib when she got home from school. His biggest smile was for her and her alone. She tried to resist, but it was no use. She fell in love with him too, and to this day my children adore each other and support each other in hundreds of ways. When I'm having trouble with my son, whether he's angry about something that happened in the schoolyard or sad because he hasn't seen his father, I try to involve my daughter. When she is having a crisis, I make sure to involve him. Not only do they depend on each other, but their love for each other has made them both feel useful.

Feeling useful is one of the great emotional stabilizers. If you know that someone else needs you, if you understand that you can help someone else, it puts you in touch with the rest of humanity and brings your own problems into perspective. I tell my daughter that she has helped me raise my son, and she has. The truth is that they have brought out the best in each other. Watching this has given me more pleasure and satisfaction than I ever imagined a human being could experience.

THE MORNING of my son's tenth birthday, the mother of a boy who had not been invited to his birthday party called to ask what my son wanted as a gift. I had to decide whether to tell the mother that her child wasn't invited, or to tell my son that he had to invite the child to his birthday party. I had to decide whether I would have enough cake for an extra boy, and whether my patience would extend to entertaining another ten-year-old in my living room. I decided to let the child come. It seemed the right thing to do. At lunchtime I walked over to my son's school and told him what had happened. "We'll deal with it. It will be fine," I told him. Looking back, I see that was the right decision. At the time it was very confusing.

One of the things that makes parental instincts work is the context of the family. It's important to pay attention to the atmosphere in a household, and to create an atmosphere of gentleness and respect in which ugly fights aren't likely to happen. Such an atmosphere is a powerful force, a more powerful force than rules and regulations. We can see how this works in our own response to churches and libraries. These are places where we automatically move quietly and drop our voices to a whisper, even though no one has to tell us to do that. A visit to a church can transform a wild child into a wide-eyed spectator. When I was growing up there were some households where I was a polite girl without even trying; politeness was just in the air somehow. Then there were other households where all was chaos, and we children added to the general disorder. The atmosphere is the environment that shapes the individual. It's the nurture in "nature versus nurture."

My son goes to a school where the atmosphere inhibits teasing, disrespect, and violence of any kind. Because of this atmosphere, the school runs smoothly without bells or public address system announcements. People smile at each other in the halls. Almost everyone is willing to help—whatever the problem might be. This atmosphere has been painstakingly built by the school's principal, Shelley Harwayne, who calls it "social tone." Through small things like personal art on the walls, and big things like schoolwide meetings and letters to parents, she has created an atmosphere where it just seems natural to behave well.

For a while she carried a mug with a motto which made fun of the famous crack: "Those who can't, teach." "Those who can, teach," her mug proclaimed. "Those who can't, go into some less significant line of work." The school custodian pointed out to her that he was one of the many school employees who don't teach. "How do you think that makes me feel?" he asked.

"Needless to say, it was a revelation for me," Harwayne writes in her book about the school, *Going Public.* "I felt the blood drain from my face. I was speechless. I never intended to hurt the custodian's feelings, nor the paraprofessionals, school aides, security guards, kitchen workers, nurses, or secretaries. I know the work they do is very significant.

The school wouldn't run well without them. But I had never paused to think about the inscription on that mug from anyone else's point of view. No, I had thought of it merely as a compliment to the teaching profession. I remain grateful to John for having the courage and wisdom to teach me not to be elitist or exclusionary in a school building. You don't have to have a teaching license to make a difference in children's lives."

Once my son and a friend teased a new boy who had brought a strange-looking lunch to school—a Japanese bento box. The boys were immediately stopped and separated. A teacher asked them how they thought it felt to be teased. Their behavior was taken very, very seriously. When I hear adults say things like, "Boys will be boys" or "That's just kids being kids," I wonder if they realize how that sounds.

I try hard to create a harmonious, humorous atmosphere within our family. The first part of creating a benevolent atmosphere is creating a family in the first place. Children are searching for identity, and much of that identity can be provided by a strong sense of family. In our family, we all know our family history and we tell lots of little family stories. I am fascinated by my family, both on my mother's and on my father's sides, and I try to generate some of that fascination in my children.

I tell my children stories about our family history—about their great-grandfather who helped Alexander Graham Bell invent the telephone and their great-grandfather who ran a livery stable. I talk about my parents, and I encourage my children to ask about their fathers' parents. I often suggest to my children that certain characteristics— whether it's the shape of their feet or a quirk of their character—are inherited from me or from someone else in our family. I think that a sense of family gives children an environment, a sense of who they are, but also a sense of perspective that helps them become their best selves. We all want to belong. Family is where we do belong.

My father was good at creating family. Sometimes we all thought he went too far. He liked to make pronouncements about what members of our family did and didn't do. "Cheevers never wear overcoats," he would say, and for years I froze in the winter. "Cheevers don't care about winning," he would say. That made more sense to me. Whatever he did, it worked well. My brothers and I are not only close, but we also get along well with my mother. In dealing with our father's estate we are able to act as a unit. From speaking with friends who are lawyers, I know how rare this kind of unity can be.

In my family, we are lucky enough to have a summer place where my mother's family has been going for generations. My children love this place, less for its amenities—it is rustic, to say the least—than for its spirit. They love to hear about the time my cousins and I searched in the sparse sand of our beach for my Aunt Janey's diamond bracelet. They like to know that I was a child there, and that their grandmother brought their grandfather there when he began courting her. They like all the family stories about the time the chickens got loose or the day the pig fell into the well. It makes them feel part of a family—but there are hundreds of ways to make children feel part of family. Once they are secure in their place in their own family, they will also feel as if they are part of the human family.

In our family, I try to limit rules. I think that rules themselves in-dicate some kind of breakdown in the family atmosphere. Rules are imposed by the powerful on the powerless. They are an invitation to re-bellion. In an intelligent, humorous, and loving atmosphere, rules are not necessary. I am on time; I expect my children to be on time. I honor their anxieties; I expect them to honor my anxieties. Members of a family don't torture each other, and we all know that waiting for some-one who is late can feel like torture. Members of a family help each other. I rarely punish my children, and to me even the word punish-ment has a harsh and creepy sound. When we disagree, I try to teach my children to reason things out. I try to leave the room instead of yelling or throwing things. We are a family, I tell my kids—and I say the word family as if it were the most serious thing in the world.

MIGHT MAKES RIGHT?

PEOPLE ARE SHOCKED when I say that I have hit my daughter. When my friends heard that I was going to write about hitting my daughter, and about parents hitting their children, one of them, a lawyer, called me and advised me not to. If I wrote about this, he assured me, it might come back to haunt her. In the future, her enemies would be able to use it against her. She would be forever labeled as a battered child. He spoke as if keeping it hidden would somehow make it go away. Why is physical violence, once a commonplace in raising children, now a forbidden subject?

There is such a thing as child abuse and it is dreadful. Children are beaten, burned, and killed by their parents and by other adults in their lives. What I am writing about is something different, certainly in degree—and perhaps also in kind. I'm writing about my experience of slapping my daughter a few times when she was between the ages of six and twelve. My hand rarely made contact with her skin, but at the moment of contact I felt angrier at her—the child I love—than I have ever felt in my life. The shocking thing isn't that I slapped her. What was shocking then and is shocking now is the intensity and the suddenness of the rage I felt, rage toward a person whom I love with a sweetness which has changed my life. For years my daughter had the ability to send me from zero to sixty in a split second. Sometimes parents do lash out at children physically; this is one of the things few people discuss about modern parenting. It's no wonder that we feel guilty and confused.

One of my most vivid childhood recollections is being hit— spanked—by my own father. My father's rage was institutionalized and socially acceptable. The world was on his side. "You're going to get a spanking," he would say. I would be turned over his knees with my pants pulled down and my legs trailing on the floor. He would hit me until he wasn't angry anymore.

That was only a generation ago, and I wonder how we could all have been so innocent. In those days, spanking was a rite of passage. My parents used physical force against us without a qualm, as their parents had. My mother's father had used his belt, or a tennis racket, or any hard object which happened to be around. They considered us lucky that they only used their hands. My friends' parents sometimes used switches.

I also remember the last spanking my father threatened me with, when I was about eleven years old. He advanced toward me across the living room, his voice vibrating with rage. Instead of submitting, I ran. I had had it. The idea of being humiliated and hurt once again was just overwhelming. I didn't think. When I saw him coming, I ducked back into my bedroom and tore through the bathroom and out the other side with my father in pursuit. I vaulted over the sofa, tumbled on the floor, and scrambled back up at a run. He was right behind me as I slammed out the front door and raced into the woods.

Hours later, when I finally returned home, he had calmed down. "I guess you're too old to be spanked anymore," he said—as if he had decided this on some kind of rational basis. My defiance against my parents—and all the rules that grown-ups thought were so impor- tant—got a big boost that day. "One of the worst side effects of physi- cal punishment is that it may interfere with the development of a child's conscience. Spanking relieves guilt too easily: the child, having paid for his misbehavior, feels free to repeat," writes Haim Ginott in *Between Parent and Child*. "Children develop what Selma Fraiberg calls a book- keeping approach to misconduct: it permits them to misbehave and thus go into debt on one side of the ledger, and pay off in weekly or monthly spanking installments."

One of our biggest jobs as parents is to help our children develop a conscience. Without an internal ethical gyroscope, they will be lost. Any kind of extreme punishment—particularly physical punishment—can interrupt that development. The seductive thing about punishment is that it works, at least on the surface. My parents thought that when my father spanked me for stealing chocolate, I never stole chocolate again. The truth was quite different. The truth was that I made sure that they never caught me stealing chocolate again. Through punishment, they created a kind of war game in which the real crime was getting caught. I never worried for a second about whether there was something wrong with stealing. The punishment disconnected the act of theft from my emerging awareness that theft was wrong. By punishing they didn't keep me from stealing, they simply made me into a much more skillful thief.

Somewhere between my childhood and now, hitting became completely off limits for thoughtful parents. These days few parents like to admit that they use physical force on their children. When my son was in nursery school, I asked a weekly meeting of nursery school mothers about this. Slowly, painfully, they began to talk about hitting their children. Even more slowly they began to confess to having been hit as children themselves. It seemed to me that women who had been hit, or women who admitted to having been hit, were more likely to hit their children. This is what the studies say. "In the olden days children were spanked plenty and nobody thought about it," writes Dr. Spock, the authority on being good parents in more recent olden days. His revered book on parenting went through revision after revision as attitudes changed and changed again and again. "Then a reaction set in and many parents decided it was shameful. But that didn't settle everything." Spock can hardly control his view, which was the view of the generation he came from—sometimes nothing but physical punishment will do.

The new generation's Penelope Leach is gentler. "Small children learn their behavior partly from parents, so you have to ask yourself whether you want your child to learn that violence is a legitimate way to make a point." From me this gets the old yes and no answer. Of course I don't want my children to think that violence is a way to make a point. Certainly few parents would answer that they do. We all know that violence is bad and peaceful reasoning is good. Nevertheless, there is plenty of violence in our world. There is violence on television and violence in video games and violence in song lyrics and violence in the schoolyard. Furthermore we live in a world where large numbers of people *do* use violence to make a point. This is true of many situations, ranging from a street mugging to the United States government foreign policy. The violence on television is not restricted to grade B movies or the Cartoon Network or *Beavis and Butt-head*. It is also a steady subject on CNN and the news channels. My son has a friend whose father is teaching him karate. "I want him to be able to defend himself," the father tells me. I don't train my children for physical combat. I try to teach them to avoid dangerous situations. I know that they may not always be able to. I wonder if they should be taking karate.

IT DOESN'T MATTER what the experts say. My rage against my daughter—whether it results in a slap or just angry words—leaves me feeling ashamed and guilty and horrified at my own behavior. I slapped her once when a baby-sitter was in the kitchen. When she ran into the kitchen crying, the baby-sitter laughed it off. "My mom gives me a slap all the time!" she said, laughing. "And she slaps hard!" She almost seemed proud of her mother's strength. I, sunk in self-hatred because of my loss of control, envied her lightheartedness.

This rage against my child used to catch me completely by surprise, like a force five blast of wind. Suddenly, usually over nothing, I would be possessed by an anger so irrational that nothing could stop it. Count to ten? There was not even a heartbeat between the thought and the action when this happened. There was the provocation—usually a messy room or tangled hair or some other globally important problem—and there was the slap.

That I can feel this intense fury at a child I love so passionately is one of the most disturbing mysteries of parenting. My daughter is precious. I would do anything to keep her from harm, to save her from the slightest pain. My brother says that he'll load his kids into the car with their mother, wanting to kill them, and then start worrying, the minute they are out of the driveway, that they might get hurt. I know what he's saying.

Here's the thing, though. I can analyze this paradox for pages. I can speculate that this only happens between mothers and daughters, and then I can explore why that might be true. There is one thing I know absolutely and that is this: the violence of a slap is compounded when it becomes a shameful secret. Violence may be wrong, but secrecy always increases any wrong. That's what I told the lawyer who urged me not to write about children and physical violence. Being a parent is confusing and difficult, but it doesn't have to be filled with private humiliations and inhibitions.

I believe that most parenting problems arise because the parent hasn't grown up yet. Since the parent is still a child, it's impossible to take on the kind of authority that children crave and require. One of the things that happen is that they abuse the authority they have. That's what breaks my heart about this hitting issue. After I escaped from my father that day, I never took him seriously again. He made our relationship into a contest—a contest of wills and a contest of speed. I won. End of story.

When I have slapped my daughter, or when I have been angrier at her than she deserves, I immediately apologize. I offer to talk about it— and we have talked about this issue a lot. No matter how often I lose control, I am the parent in our equation and I know that when authority is brittle it often just shatters into pieces. I want my daughter to understand that although I make mistakes—and I make plenty—that doesn't mean that I am no longer in charge. I am in charge of supporting her financially and emotionally, and I am also in charge of our household. It's not a contest or a battleground.

AT THE SAME TIME, the right kind of authority for parents to wield over their children is hard to define, and it changes from day to day and from situation to situation. Children change so fast that often, by the time I have come up with a solution to a problem, they have grown out of the problem. I try not to be arbitrary. If my son or daughter makes me angry, I try to explain why. If they want something that I can't afford, I explain why we can't afford it and suggest that we make some kind of savings plan so that we might be able to afford it someday. This is easy for me since I am the parent who makes the money, keeps the books, and pays the bills. I also try not to buy anything for myself that we can't afford.

If one of my children is disrupting our lives together—by doing anything from swearing to staying out late to spilling glue on the furniture—I explain why they have to stop. I also try to be sure that I don't disrupt our lives together. I don't think that we were all put on earth to torture each other. I try not to do things that torture my children. These things can range from talking about them to other adults to staying out later than I have promised, and I encourage them to tell me if I am. I also try to be sure that they don't do things which torture me.

In the end, though, although my children often argue with me, and beg and whine and plead, they know that they do not argue as equals. Our family is not a democracy. My children are not afraid to ask me for anything, but they know that I am not afraid to tell them that the answer is no. They know that if they break their promises to me, consequences will be swift. These consequences can range from a freeze on toys, to a cutback on swimming trips, to a complete loss of privileges.

I try to make the punishment fit the crime—but I try even harder to make the punishment fit the family. A few Sundays ago, a father I know lost patience with his sons and—before he had time to think— he had sent them both to their rooms for the day. He lives in a small apartment, and as we talked on the telephone I could hear his boys wailing and screaming in the background. Who was getting punished in that situation? I don't like to think about what kind of day that family had.

That's the essence of being a grown-up to me: not being afraid to lead even though I may not always lead well. Being the boss is scary, especially in an endeavor as tricky as raising children. I may be wrong as often as I'm right—but I'm not afraid to give it my best try. I listen carefully to my children, but I try to give them the benefit of my larger perspective and my decades of experience—whether they want it or not. The nature of being a child is to think you know what's best for you— and to be mistaken at least as often as your parents are mistaken.

How can we go about creating a loving authority for our children, an authority that teaches them how to live and keeps our families in balance, but which is also flexible and humorous enough to bend and stretch and avoid the kind of direct confrontation that will destroy it? This was not the kind of authority our parents inherited. They were whipped if they disobeyed. Their schools were more like prisons than playgrounds. They were supposed to behave like miniature adults, and when they couldn't they were banished. "Children should be seen and not heard," was my great-grandmother's maxim and the truth was that she would just as soon the children weren't seen either.

Then during the time I was growing up, parents and children alike discovered freedom, as if it was a rich vein of gold in a mine where we had been hacking away for years with dull picks. Parents threw away their discipline and their rules. Bedtime became a dirty word. Schedules were for trains. Schools abandoned their curriculums. Children were taught to be themselves, to follow their own interests, to invent their own educations. When children misbehaved, they were asked about their motives.

As a student, I was delirious with pleasure when this happened. I had always hated rules. I, who had been almost kicked out of school for talking in the halls and not sitting still at Study Hall, found myself at the Woodstock Country School where no one cared where I worked— they only cared about the quality of the work. Now that made sense! This school specialized in imaginative punishments. When a group of students stole all the flatware from the cafeteria as a prank, the school's headmaster responded perfectly. At an assembly he explained that everyone would eat with their fingers until the flatware was returned. Privately he suggested the week's menus to the kitchen staff. The flatware was back within a day.

After graduating from college, I became a teacher in just such an alternative school. I taught high school for three years, and after a twenty-year break, I went back to teaching college and graduate students six years ago. In my first years of teaching I also believed that rules and regulations were bad for the soul. I thought that children should have the freedom to learn at their own pace in their own way. I was as much a student as I was a teacher, and in some ways this was very successful. My students taught me how to ski. My tenth-grade boys helped me repaint my room. I taught at a school which set great store by physical adventures, and on these adventures—hiking across glaciers or spelunking in the great caves of the West—my students were able to teach me. There, they were authorities. My students held the belay ropes as I rappelled down a cliff. They taught me about the outdoors.

Because we had a kind of parity, I was able to teach them about books and poetry. I saw young men who had thought poetry was for sissies suddenly understand a poet like William Butler Yeats. I thought the key to teaching was to abdicate the fortress of phony authority which had been built up over years of educational traditions. It's as a parent that I've been brought up short: my treasured ideas about education and the importance of abdicating unjust and artificial authority don't work very well in parenting. What I think my children should want and need just doesn't seem to correspond with what my children obviously want and need.

I don't impose meaningless schedules and strictures on my kids, but they are hungry for rules. If I don't make rules, they make them up for themselves. I hate the idea of a set bedtime, but without it my children don't feel safe at night. They need to argue about whether they can stay up, and they need to lose . . . most of the time. It's a ritual. They have requested menus, so that every Sunday night is pizza night and so on throughout the week. They want to know exactly what's going to happen each day, and I try and tell them.

To me freedom is a fundamental human right—*the* fundamental human right. Freedom, as we guarantee it in the First Amendment to the Constitution, is what makes our country great. Freedom to write what we want, freedom to speak our minds is as precious as anything on earth. I like to quote what Yeats wrote about Jonathan Swift, that "he served human liberty. Imitate him if you dare!" But freedom is for grown-ups. My kids don't care about Yeats and Swift and the First Amendment to the Constitution of the United States. They want their days to follow in ritual succession, and they want to know what's going to happen next. They want order. They want a home where the rules—kept by them and by me—are their bulwark against the chaos of the world we live in.

TEACHER VERSUS PARENT

LIKE GOVERNMENTS, we parents are charged with the responsibility of representing our little constituents on the one hand, and balancing their individual welfare with the common good of the whole family on the other hand. Our constituents should go to bed on time because they need their sleep, but they should also go to bed so that their parents can have some precious hours alone. I often joke that our family is a lot like a small unruly banana republic, with me, the mother, as the benevolent dictator. The truth is that as a member of our family's governing body—in my case the only member of our family's governing body—my real model is Niccolo Machiavelli. The book he titled *The Prince* could just as easily be titled *The Parent*. If there ever was a situation in which the ends should justify the means, it's the situation of parents raising children.

Parenting is about power. Children have no economic power, little intellectual power, and not much physical power. The only power they have is that we love them; otherwise, they are helpless. Successful parenting requires a successful wielding of our power in a way that is both hidden and tolerant—but also effective. We must listen to our children; we *must* listen to them. Listening looks quiet, but it is a powerful action. We must hear our children when they share their reactions, their desires, their likes and dislikes. Just as important, we must teach them to listen to us and to other people in the world around them. Parental power is so complicated, so murky and obscured by intense feelings, that it's hard to see how simple it can be. In order to use our power effectively, not ignoring it and not abusing it, we have to leave our own childhoods behind and become adults ourselves.

As a teacher, for instance, I have power in the classroom. My power there is automatic. My students pay to listen to me. I can affect their lives with the grades I give them and with the reports I write for them. At the same time, I have very little power over my students. If they don't like the way I teach, they can just walk out and take another course. I'll never see them again. It happens all the time. No big deal. In fact the power I do have is one of the many things that makes teaching fun. A colleague of mine, after two weeks teaching a graduate seminar, told me how shocked she was when she went home and no one laughed at her jokes. Surrounded by attentive students, she had come to think of herself as a great wit.

My power over my students usually works well for all of us. It's a balance of power that is extremely effective for the business at hand. If I were teaching my students table manners, or how to have neat rooms, or how to remember to brush their teeth, or how to tie their shoelaces, they would learn quickly and efficiently. How can it be then that I've spent hours during the last year trying to teach my son to floss and brush his teeth every morning—using every teaching skill at my command—and he still doesn't do it? Sometimes he'll go into the bathroom and run the water. Once he made a spider web by stringing the floss between the sink and the shower and back again. Sometimes he'll make a hawking sound and spit loudly into the sink. Occasionally he'll brush a tooth or two. If I put the energy into a student's work that I have spent trying to get my daughter to pick up her room—that student would probably read and write like an angel.

I have much more power over my children than I do over my students, but somehow that power is a liability. We get tangled up in it. As a teacher, I'm happy to exert my authority and I don't mind being disliked. As a mother I want to be both loved and obeyed. When it comes to teaching my children, the stakes are too high to let anything be simple. Everything is a big deal. This is why most children can learn faster from a stranger, someone who doesn't care so much, than they can learn from their parents, who are desperately involved in their children's learning process.

Then there's the difficulty of sharing authority with my children's fathers, a difficulty which is as real for me as a single mother as it was when I was married. There are many places where we disagree. My son's father dislikes all rules, and he likes to say that he doesn't believe in time. This drives me nuts. My daughter's father is always punctual, but he tends to be a pessimist, especially when it comes to money. My daughter is brilliant, but her father used to say sometimes that she shouldn't apply to a good college because we couldn't afford it. Every time he said this, I wanted to stop up her ears.

In the classroom, I don't have to share my authority with anyone. The students have no father teacher to correspond to my mother teacher. And at home, my children can't just walk out and find another teacher if they don't like the way I teach. We are stuck with each other for life.

There's another problem too. My authority over my children is anything but automatic. They had no choice in the matter, as they often remind me. Furthermore, the parents of my generation are reinventing parenthood as we go along. We are learning on the job. We don't have the certainties our parents did, and usually we don't have the time either. We don't have their unquestioned authority. We don't use the disciplinary tools they used. That's why teaching students is fun— everyone knows what their role is and everyone plays it—and teaching my own children gives me headaches and often results in angry words and hurt feelings. It shouldn't be that way. I love my children desperately. I'll probably never see most of my students after graduation. I think that teaching my children would be easier if I brought more Machiavellian distance and trickery to the gigantic task of transforming children into adults. As long as we are still children, our ability to teach our own children will be inhibited by that. In the classroom I'm clearly the adult. At home, I am trying to be the adult.

STEPMOTHER

MY FIRST EXPERIENCES as a stepmother were disastrous. At twenty-three I married a man seven years older than I was. He may not have been Mr. Right, I used to say, but he was certainly Mr. Willing. He had already been married, and he was the father of two rambunctious, beautiful daughters aged three and five. In those days—it was 1967—women were expected to get married as soon as possible and to be literally handed at the altar from father to husband. Women weren't supposed to grow up and get jobs and take responsibility—they were supposed to get men to do that. Trying to deal with my own expectations—that my husband would take care of me; the children's expectations—that when he got over me, my husband would go back to their mother; his expectations—that I would somehow morph into a version of their mother who loved him—was the emotional equivalent of a double root canal. The only people who got hurt worse than I did were the two little girls.

I had no idea how to be a mother anyway. My own mother was a beautiful, talented woman. Her mother had died—a painful death from a long illness—when my mother was a girl, leaving a dreadful wound which was passed down through generations. In my mother's world, women had their children young. Then they got on with the business of being glamorous and witty accoutrements to their husbands' talents—the main business of their lives. In that world, children really were supposed to be seen and not heard, but that wasn't all. When children were seen, they were expected to say please and thank you, to call all adults Mister and Missus in a particularly obsequious tone of voice, to behave impeccably, and—as my father used to say—to "look like something."

I had no desire to be a mother myself, certainly not when I married at twenty-three. My mother used to tell me a story about the day I was born, a day when she was twenty-three. She was walking along Eighth Street in Greenwich Village, a few hours before she went to the hospital. My father was away in the army. It was the end of July. It was hot. It was hotter than hot. The pavements were steaming. She saw a woman pulling a young child into a movie theater. The child was dressed in a cotton shift and she was barefoot. She didn't want to go. The woman pulled. The child resisted. Finally the woman's superior strength prevailed and the child was pulled into the darkness. Even as a child I could figure out what that story meant about my mother's reluctance to have a child.

During our courtship, there had been no children in evidence. We dated for a summer and then corresponded. He said not a word about his children. Sometime that fall, he asked me to come back to New York and move in with him. This was a very bohemian request in those days. My parents disapproved; his parents disapproved. I still hadn't met his two little girls. I said yes. Before we married, I met them once or twice. They seemed noisy and destructive. They broke my husband's most precious things, jumped up and down in his lap, ate all the ice cream in the freezer, and made reasonable conversation impossible. Their demands seemed incessant. Nothing was safe from them.

I assumed that, after their visits, when they finally left to go back to their mother, my husband was as relieved as I was. When they were with us, I counted the hours. I imagined that when he came from taking them back to their mother, he felt as if he could walk on air. He was angry sometimes when he got home, and who could blame him? His ex-wife was impossible. That's why he had divorced her. I assumed he was irritated because of the way she dumped the kids on us. Who in their right mind would want to have their very pleasant life regularly shattered by crying, whining, demanding, expensive little people who were, after all, the unfair and huge result of an early mistake? He often said he should never have married his first wife. I assumed this meant that he felt they should never have had children. I was terribly wrong.

It didn't seem fair that in marrying the man I loved I also seemed to have married his children and even his ex-wife and, on some days, her new boyfriend. I didn't understand why his children should be my problem. "I didn't marry your children," became my mantra. Didn't they already have a mother? When the girls were with us—on the classic Wednesday night and alternate weekend schedule mandated by divorce—I tried to assume parental authority. I got them haircuts. I washed their clothes, and threw out the ones that looked worn-out. I made them go to bed at set times so that we could have a quiet dinner—this was my idea of what constituted parental authority. I had virtually no experience of parental authority.

As our marriage lasted and moved forward, we moved from the city to the country, then we moved from the country to another country. My husband was eager for children of our own. I could hardly suppress my scorn at this idea. Didn't we have enough trouble with the children he had already had? Even living abroad, we had to send a monthly check back to New York to support them. We would never be free. The last thing we needed was more children. His children made me painfully uncomfortable, and my only respite was their absence. If I was stupid enough to have a child of my own, there would be no respite—that's what I thought.

MY SECOND SET of stepchildren were older when I met their father. My first marriage had slowly faded until it became nothing but an inconvenience as far as I was concerned. In those days divorce was just another rite of passage, and I was eager to experience it. I had friends who threw themselves divorce parties—on the theory that there was more to celebrate in a divorce (mutual freedom) than there ever was in a marriage (mutual bondage). It was the 1970s, and having children was what people did in the suburbs. In New York we were slick and cool and we had discovered the joys of sex, the joys of drugs, the joys of working, the joys of living alone, the joys of not being like our parents' tied-down, hidebound generation. Age didn't matter, money didn't matter, the old rules didn't matter.

Still, my new husband had children—he had them back in the dark ages when everyone did—and our rare times with his children often ended with bitter fights. He was older than I was and his children were in their twenties, but that didn't make them want to be close to me. They had been through a divorce already. They were the children of his first wife; I was his third wife. I was amazed and offended by their loyalty to his ex-wife, a woman who wasn't even their mother. She had been their stepmother for fifteen years. I heard that they hadn't liked her much then. Now they visited her and talked about her and worried about her. My husband had left her for me, and they seemed to hold this against me. This seemed very unfair. They were adults, after all. This was the way of the world. I hadn't exactly invented adultery all by myself.

Furthermore, I didn't see why I couldn't be honest about their failings; was I supposed to lie? I criticized them as freely as I criticized any adults whom I found wanting—and that was many adults. They were actually estimable men and women, but at times they dressed strangely, and they lived in out-of-the-way places. I was always amazed that when I criticized one of his children, my husband acted as if I was speaking about *his* failings. "When you criticize them, it goes through me like a knife," he said.

I just didn't get it. Before I had a child, I had no idea what all the fuss was about. Children were so noisy, and they were such a lot of trouble. When children were around, everyone seemed to change, to go a little crazy or to get very angry. When it came to understanding the human family—the human condition—I was in the dark. I remember being in my gynecologist's office one morning with three impressively beautiful professional women. They wore gleaming low heels and carried authoritative briefcases. They had thick hair cut short or pulled back in buns. I was in sweat pants and a T-shirt. Then a baby appeared, crawling ahead of its mother on the carpet. The three women dropped their poses and hit the floor cooing and goo-gooing and chuckling over the baby. I thought they were ridiculous.

• • •

Now my children have stepmothers. As a mother who watched her precious child be driven away in a young woman's sports car for her weekend with her father, I began to see what kind of stepmother I had been. I knew that the driver of that sports car had no idea of the preciousness of her cargo. Not only did I compete with my stepchildren— after all, I was a child myself—but I completely failed to understand the feelings of their real mother. The children's importance to her was beyond my comprehension. For me, good stepparenting was impossible until I had a child of my own. I didn't know what a family was. The idea of putting aside my own welfare for a common good was completely alien.

The feelings which are at the basis of any love—the acceptance, the unselfishness—were not on my screen. We live in a country where the individual is in the ascendant, and we seem to believe that our individual destinies are more important than anything else. It's a high romantic ideal, this American way, an ideal of the value of each person's freedom. I had embraced that ideal in order to rationalize my own self-absorption. The birth of my daughter ended that.

Liley was a perfect child, and her perfection seemed like an enormous gift. I knew that I had done nothing to deserve such a gift. That was part of what blew away the straitjacket of self-absorption in which I had been living. Watching my baby girl, as I did for hours, I would pinch myself in disbelief. How had I come to possess, to be in the company of such a beautiful child? I was in love with her, and I was also in awe of her—or of whoever had created her. She was everything I was not. She was perfect evidence of God's grace. In coming to love her, I learned to love the world.

As my baby and I got to know each other, as she cried less and smiled more, and as I began to trust my own maternal intuition—I was electrified by fear. Before I had her, I didn't really care what happened to me, or to anyone else for that matter. Now the thought of anything happening to my daughter, a scratch or an accident, sent me into a cold sweat. She was very, very sick as a child. I sleepwalked through her illnesses in a kind of numb terror.

When she was three days old, we had to return to the hospital.

The pediatric wards of hospitals are strange, twilit places. There are great heros there and great tragedies, and everyone's walking around in a caul of mortal fear. Twice, during Liley's first two years, she spent a week in the hospital. Once she had a tremor that no one could diagnose. I stayed with her, on a foldout bed at Lenox Hill and on a cot next to her bed at Mount Sinai. She got better. Another time she had pneumonia. I lay next to her and prayed.

My fear in the hospitals wasn't the worst of it, though; the worst of it was the return to normal life—not that I would ever return to normal life, really. When she moved into her own room at age one, she seemed to take my heart with her. She was too far away. The world was too dangerous for me to bear her vulnerability in it. Inside there were knives, electricity, dry cleaner bags, water, and windows with flimsy child guards. Outdoors there were serial killers, drug dealers, cars, rabid dogs, and don't even get me started on germs.

Somehow my daughter picked up on my fears. By the time she was two, she found the idea of her father and me going out at night absolutely unacceptable. At the appearance of a suitcase, or a party dress, or if she overheard me blow-drying my hair, she would begin to wail. She was a remarkably articulate little girl. She would wrap her tiny arms around my ankles and sob. "Please don't go, please." When I tried to reason with her, her anguish increased. "Don't leave me here with the baby-sitter!" she would begin to howl. "I know something bad will happen. I can feel it! Something bad will happen. Please don't go!"

By this time, of course, she had convinced me that a disaster was imminent. You can call this preaching to the converted, but it was more like shrieking to the shrieks that were already coming from my inner fears. My intuition told me to stay home, to take the easy way out. Often I did, but slowly I began to see that my daughter's howls were really a question, a question about the safety of the world and the likelihood that, if I left the room, I would come back.

Some of the worst times in my life have been the endless minutes when I walked down the hallway and left my apartment with my daughter's abandoned screams receding in the distance. I learned that, as painful as it seemed, I didn't have to share her fears. I could leave, and that would show her that people who left did usually come back. I tell my children that I will keep them safe. That's what parents tell their kids, I think. Of course it's not strictly true—only God can really keep anyone safe—but what I mean is that I am going to do everything I can to keep them safe and to be sure that they are safe with me.

In college psychology classes they used to tell us that the mark of maturity was the ability to accept delayed gratification. The adult was the person who would choose to have a big chocolate bar tomorrow rather than a small one today. I think what they meant was that being an adult means a faith in the future—the faith that tomorrow will actually happen, that good work will have good results, and that people who go out for dinner will be there when you wake up in the morning. I didn't want to be an adult, but now that I was a mother, there wasn't room in our family for another child.

PLEASE DON'T Go!

I HAVE COME TO BELIEVE that the three basic tools of parenting are: bribery, extortion, and threats. There are many experts who complain that once a parent begins bribing a child, a "bad precedent" has been set. I respectfully disagree. Perhaps the problem is with the connotations of baksheesh in Third World countries. Call it what you will, bribing my children with gifts and with money—as we are all "bribed" by our friends and employers—has been one of my most successful techniques as a parent. I began discovering this in dealing with my toddler daughter's acute separation anxiety.

When she sobbed out her fears on the floor, or at the door to the elevator, I would quietly interrupt her. "What would you like me to bring you?" I would ask. "Would you like me to bring you a cookie from the dinner? Would you like me to buy you a toy in Boston?" The sobs would almost always be replaced by contemplation. Fear is easily dispelled by desire, and desire drags us into the future. "Ahhh," my husband would say. "The lamp of acquisition has been lit!"

The worst of the separation traumas my daughter and I grew up through was the trauma of her going to school. Each school has its own rules about whether or not parents of nursery school children are allowed to hang around after school begins. Some ban parents; some welcome them. Fortunately the school my daughter went to was welcoming. At first she went to the kind of school where I or her baby-sitter stayed with her, or sat out in the hall while she romped and colored with her peers.

When it was time to go to a real school—she was two years old at this point—I applied to a nursery school in a narrow town house on 92nd Street. I took her up there for testing. The test, for a two-year-old, consisted of a variety of puzzles and wooden cutout games, but it seemed to be taken every bit as seriously as the SATs and law boards my friends and I had taken years earlier. A teacher administered the test in carefully controlled conditions. One was a puzzle of vegetable and fruit pieces. "Which of these would a guinea pig be most likely to eat?" the tester asked in a low, intense voice. Liley paused for a moment. "Do guinea pigs eat puzzle pieces?" she asked.

I remember those early days of her schooling vividly even now, more than a decade later. All the other mothers would leave. Sometimes there were a few tears, a brief promise, and then departure. My daughter wouldn't let me go, and she wouldn't even think of letting me go. I sat in a child-sized chair and tried to start her on a project, any project. The room was narrow with windows at either end, looking into a garden in the back and looking into the street in the front. Other children waved happily at the window at their retreating parents.

"Sit down!" my daughter would say in a voice that admitted no negotiation. It was hard for me not to glance outside at the other adults savoring their freedom as I bent over construction paper and glue, trying to distract my child from my departure. I tried everything, coloring, a picture book, a set of building blocks. She would play happily by my side, but the moment I pushed back my chair she would grab me, grab my clothes, and begin to scream. "Mommy, don't go!"

I was mortified, but I stayed, often with rising anger. Her clinginess made me crazy; probably because she was daring to express the fears that had ruled my life. Why did I have to have the kid who wouldn't let their mother go? Why did I have to be the sap who hung around and played coloring games and got to know the teachers? The situation broke my heart and made me furious—simultaneously. It was one of those teachers who kindly suggested that I might want to have someone else bring my daughter to school. I was outraged. Who would console her then for the loss? She wouldn't need to be consoled, this teacher said, because there wouldn't be any loss. I was the cause of my child's anxieties as well as the—not very successful—cure.

My daughter always loved her bottle, and she liked to take it to school. The teacher outlawed it. Slowly I weaned her off her daytime bottle until she just had one, at night. One of my own mother's most often repeated stories is about taking my bottle away from me when I was a year old. My mother blames this on the pediatrician. The pediatrician scared her, she says. She took my bottle away. I cried for days. I replaced the bottle with my thumb. My daughter was four years old before I took her bottle away at night. She didn't even seem to notice; in fact she seemed relieved. Someone pointed out to me that she knew perfectly well that she was too old for a bottle, and that part of my job was helping her to grow up. My own experience was irrelevant.

Parenting is a study in paradox. Whatever seems to be true in one instant—children need attention, for instance—will seem the opposite in the next—children need to be left alone sometimes. Nowhere is this paradox more vivid than in the issues of separation and attachment, attention and distraction, love and limits. As a mother, I want to protect my children, and they desperately need my protection. On the other hand there are many, many situations in which my children need to find their own way—without my protection. My daughter needed to work out her own ways of dealing with school. As long as I was there, playing with construction paper, sitting in the undersized chairs, she couldn't figure out how to adjust. I was shielding my daughter, but I was also blocking out the world.

When my son faces a difficult situation at school I can say, "I know this is a hard situation, and I will be there by your side," or I can say, "I know this is a hard situation, and I know you can handle it." Both are right.

It's the same with paying attention. Of course children need a huge amount of attention. They need to be comforted, they need to be guided, they need to be clothed and fed and almost everything else. They also need to be left alone. It took me a long time to see that sometimes when I was distracted—by my own life or crises among my friends—my children took advantage of that distraction to grow up all by themselves. When I couldn't take my daughter to school because I had something else to do, and because her teacher recommended that I have someone else take her, her problems disappeared. Because I couldn't take the time to toilet-train my son, he toilet-trained himself. When I stopped worrying about what my daughter ate, she lost weight. The maternal connection which nourishes my children can also trap them.

Mother love—whether it comes from a man or a woman—is powerful, so powerful that it can be a problem as well as a solution. My passion for Liley was so great that I truly, truly thought she was an exceptional child—one in a million. (She has turned out to be, of course!) I won't forget the day I took her to our first babies and mothers class at a school down the street. There were ten mothers and ten babies enrolled for exercise, crafts, and advice. My daughter was clearly a superior baby. I was actually amazed when the other mothers didn't drop their inferior babies and rush over to admire my baby. This isn't a joke; I was really surprised. It came as a shock to me that many mothers feel about their children the way I feel about mine—that in fact that powerful, powerful feeling is the basis for human society.

I once mentioned to my mother that I thought my infant daughter didn't love me as much as she loved her father. "Of course she doesn't love you," my mother said, "you're her earth." As a mother who came to this realization late in life, I find it intoxicating. In an unsafe world I am prepared to side with my children no matter what. I am their earth. Because my love for them is so strong and so complicated, it's sometimes hard for me to know when to stop. I can see that my presence at my daughter's side might not be appropriate, say, on her first date. That doesn't keep me from wanting to be there!

My children will have their own lives, with their own human anguish and ecstasy, and there is nothing I can do about that. As a parent, my power is limited. This is hard to accept. I love my children so much that I want to save them from all pain and assure them all happiness. I can't do that, though; I mean it won't work. I have to get out of the way. I have to remember that my help is sometimes a hindrance. This became very clear in the story of how my children were toilet-trained.

When my daughter was almost two, I decided, with some help from my pediatrician and an assortment of nannies and experts, that it was time. I bought a cute little potty. She ignored it. Over the next months I spent hours trying to get her to use the potty. I cajoled, I pleaded. For a while I bought her a present each time she complied. I spent hundreds of dollars in bribes. Finally, when she was about thirty months old—after six months of this—it worked! I patted myself on the back and congratulated myself on my parenting skills.

Then when my son turned two, I bought him a cute little potty. I felt a tremendous confidence. I knew how to toilet-train a child! Same story. But we were moving and our family was changing fast and I got distracted. The potty gathered dust in the corner of the bathroom. My son happily used diapers. I felt guilty. I knew I should be spending those hours and that bribe money "teaching" him to use the potty. I figured he'd be in diapers well into his adult life. Then, when he was about thirty months old, I found him sitting on the potty. He decided he was too big for diapers, he explained, as if he was teaching me something. Was he ever; was he ever! The light dawned. I hadn't toilet-trained my daughter, I had merely spent a ridiculous amount of time and money trying to get her to do something that she wasn't ready to do. When she was ready, it happened. I had nothing to do with it.

THERE ARE MANY THINGS I can do for my children. I can listen to them. I can make sure that I let them finish what they are saying when they are speaking to me, and that I let a few minutes go by while I am just listening. I can try not to interrupt them. I can respond to them intelligently and kindly. I can model good behavior for them, and show them its rewards. I can provide for them. There are also many things I can't do for my children. I can't work out their connection to the world around them or to their peers. Wisdom is knowing the difference between what I can and need to do as a mother, and what I can't do, and shouldn't even try to do.

I know that my son, who sometimes cries pathetically when I leave the room, will probably grow up and fall in love with another woman, and that they may get married and go on a honeymoon. I may not even be welcome. Or he may fall in love with a man. He may never fall in love at all. In promising to keep my children safe, I also have to promise that I will let go of them. Easy to say. They have introduced me to love. They have changed me from being a person trapped in my own childhood to being the adult they require as a parent. I love my children so dearly, they are never out of my thoughts. Their casual expressions and movements still astonish me, my heart leaps when I catch a glimpse of my son intently bending over his homework, his hand gripped around his pencil, or when my daughter stands in my doorway, so glad to see me that she doesn't know how to say it. In truth these feelings, the feelings I have for my children, are feelings beyond words. It's the power of these feelings, the energy generated by this, the great love of my life, that has given us the energy to create a wonderful family.

There are a lot of reasons why my children are successful, happy, good friends with each other and with the world. They succeed, to paraphrase Freud, in love and in usefulness. Their lives have not been smooth. My daughter has an eating disorder, and we have learned to deal with that a day at a time. My son has been devastated by my divorce from his father. Sometimes he has been so sad that he can't concentrate at school. We call these times sadness attacks. The things my children have—a very present mother who adores them; strict limits on behavior and reasons for those limits; a parent who has tremendous respect for their individuality; a parent who, for the most part, has left her own childhood behind—all come from the amazing, abiding love between us.

TANTRUMS

LONG BEFORE I experienced them, or anything like them—not that there is anything like them—I had read about childhood tantrums. I had read about the way young children between the ages of two and five go on crying jags which turn into full-scale displays of temper with hands and feet pounding the floor and the walls and anything else in sight. I had read that before children learn to use words to express themselves, their frustration can literally possess them.

Nevertheless, nothing could have prepared me for the experience of a child of mine having a tantrum. Nothing could have prepared me for what it's like to have the most precious person on earth suddenly throw themselves into a rage—a rage that blocks out any efforts to help, a rage which cannot see beyond itself, a rage so dreadful and painful that it wipes out all reason and all natural urges to be safe, a suicidal rage. Tantrums made me understand what people in other cultures were talking about when they thought that a child was possessed by the devil or by some other angry spirit.

One of the most frightening things about children's tantrums is their utter irrationality. By the time my daughter was enrolled in nursery school, each weekday morning had become a physical and psychological struggle during which her father and I—two healthy, intelligent, and bewildered adults—were occupied for more than an hour in

the process of getting her dressed. My daughter desperately wanted to
go to school. She loved school. She adored her teacher. But she even
more desperately did not want to get dressed to go to school. She hated
getting dressed. Clothes were her jailors and shoes were little prisons.
Somehow, the brain synapses which might have helped her understand
that in order to go to school she had to get dressed to go to school, had
not yet been developed.

It wasn't that I insisted that she wear anything special. I would
have done anything I could to help. I spent hours trying to explain that
people can't go outdoors in the winter with no shoes on. My regulations about clothes—or should I say my preferences—were immediately blown away by the magnitude of my beloved little girl's feelings.
She, on the other hand, had developed a rigid dress code which could
not be violated in any respect, and which often changed drastically
from day to day. One day, for example, she had to wear a pink dress with
matching tights.

Even if, miraculously, I was able to provide the right dress and
tights, things could still go terribly wrong. If there was a hole in the
tights, forget it. Does it sound as if she was spoiled? I don't think so. She
seemed to be in the grip of something much larger than her own desires, and much, much larger than mine. She seemed to be the victim of
her rigidity and her perfectionism as much as, or not more than, we
were. Some draconian internal need was driving her, not a desire to
manipulate her hapless parents.

On mornings when her idea of what she would wear coincided
perfectly with what was available, she could begin the dressing process
in relative calm. Before long, something inevitably went wrong. Her
shoes had a spot on them. She didn't like the feeling of the dress slipping on over her head; she hated the feeling of the dress slipping on
over her head. She didn't want to step into the dress, because she already
had her shoes on. My husband would try to distract her by telling stories, imitating animals, or making funny noises with his mouth and
nose, while I hastily tried to slip on the dress.

By the time I was halfway through, his ability to distract had usually worn off and we were in trouble again. The demons were back.
Prone on the floor, howling at the top of her lungs as if she had lost the
most valuable thing in the world, she would pound her tiny fists into

the carpet to protest the fact that she had to wear a coat. "It's freezing outside, it's snowing," I would croon. "Everyone is wearing a coat." Sometimes, by leading her to the window I could convince her that everyone was indeed wearing a coat. Usually, though, it was impossible to get through to her. And this wasn't even a full-fledged tantrum. During a full-fledged tantrum, all control is lost by the child—and often also by the parent. In this case a parent's principal job, all the experts agree, is to keep the child from hurting herself during a time when rage just seems to lift a child right out of her body.

My daughter's most memorable tantrum took place at the fancy third birthday party of a girl her age who happened to be the daughter of a famous writer. My daughter was always afraid of masks, clowns, or any kind of disguise. Halloween was a nightmare. We locked the door and didn't answer the bell, but even the idea of people with masks standing outside our door often sent my daughter into a tailspin. At this particular party, as the literary elite ate finger sandwiches and chatted over their children's headbanded and neatly barretted heads, the famous author arrived dressed as Santa Claus with a bulging bag of gifts for the lucky assembled children.

My daughter started to cry. "Ho, ho, ho!" said the author, a kind and talented man whose only thought was to please his daughter and her friends. My daughter started to whimper and pressed her head against me. "Ho, ho, ho," said Santa. My daughter started to scream. "Out! Out!" she screamed, catching her baby breath in a long sob and letting it out in another loud scream. The room was crowded with my illustrious friends and colleagues, and the only exit was the door on the opposite wall. As my daughter's screams became shrieks, I wrestled her—struggling against me—around the edge of the party. Other parents made way for us; I felt completely alone. "Out!" my beloved girl shrieked, pulling at my hair and tearing at my sweater in fear. She didn't relax until we were safely in a taxi cab. When I told the driver what had happened, he laughed. "I used to be afraid of masks myself," he said. I felt human for the first time in an hour.

Even when they happen at home, tantrums seem to happen at the worst possible times. Once, as bath time stretched into bedtime, my three-year-old son wanted to stay in the tub. I left him there for a while, until the bathwater was gray and cold and a ring of scum had formed.

Finally, over what seemed like a mild protest on his part, I reached over and pulled the plug. He began to cry, softly and sadly, as if the cold, dirty water had been an old, dear friend, as if he had somehow become deeply attached to it during their time together in the bath.

As the water gurgled down the drain, my son's sobs got louder until they reached a hysterical pitch as the last of the water disappeared. By that time he was splayed against the wet, slippery bottom of the tub, howling with grief at the loss of his beloved bathwater. Or perhaps he was howling at his own helplessness, at the agony of living in a world where someone else decides so very, very many things that you care about, including how long you get to sit in the tub with your bathwater intact.

My attempts to coax him out of the tub were barely heard over his stricken wails. Because our tub has glass shower doors, and because its porcelain sides were slippery, I was unable to remove him by force. When I tried to pull him out, he grabbed the faucets and held on, howling all the time. Terrified that he would slip and hit his head, I stood paralyzed at the door of the bathroom, ready to sob myself. This state of affairs lasted forever. Then the telephone rang.

In spite of my fears for my son, I answered the telephone. My daughter was walking home from school, and I was afraid that she might need me even more than he did. Instead it was a friend. Before I could tell her that I couldn't talk, she had launched into a litany of anxiety, and as I listened I saw my son, damp and naked, streaking out the bathroom door and toward the safety of his own room. By the time I got off the phone, he was curled up on my bed in a nest of wet towels, calmly watching the Cartoon Network.

That was when I realized that a tantrum is a dialogue somehow. The child is possessed, but his possession is directed at the parent. Break the connection and the tantrum ends. Many books suggest that when a child has a tantrum it's a good idea to leave the room. I have spent hours in my room with the door closed pretending to read while a child has a tantrum. We are still connected; I am still listening; the tantrum is still at the center of both our lives. They know I am waiting. I know they are suffering. When the telephone rings, even if it's a trivial call, a third party enters the equation. The electricity between parent and child—which goes so wrong during a tantrum—is cut. The tantrum ends.

When tantrums are in public places, as they often are, weathering them is more difficult. It's as if feelings are more likely to get out of control when we are far from home. Late one summer afternoon—late afternoons are prime time for tantrums—my son and I were coming home together on the train from a visit to the country. We had lunch at my brother's house where my son played with his cousins—also his closest and favorite friends.

When the train pulled into Grand Central, my four-year-old son said he was hungry. Accordingly, still traveling under the impression that we were two rational loving people on our way home from a country weekend, I guided him up the ramp into the central part of the station with its marble floors and high starry ceilings, and down toward a delicatessen near Lexington Avenue. The counter was one of those glass cases with three perfectly round chocolate cakes sitting on the top level. My son said he wanted cake. It was late in the afternoon, but still an hour before dinner. I agreed.

I asked the man behind the counter to cut my son a slice of chocolate cake. "Do you have any milk?" I said, feeling very generous.

"No," my son interrupted, "I want cake."

"I know," I said. "He's getting you cake."

"No, cake. Cake!" my son exclaimed. I realized that he wanted an entire chocolate cake. He didn't want the cake to be cut. He didn't want a slice of cake. He wanted the cake. He pointed at the cake he wanted, which was the middle one on the shelf. The man took the cake out, put it on the counter, and started to slice out a piece.

"Nooo." My son was crying now. "Cake!" Not only did he want the whole, beautiful cake, but the thought of having the cake sliced into pieces was somehow terribly painful for him. In retrospect it seems to me I should have bought the whole cake and taken it home in a box. I didn't know that then. I wasn't thinking fast enough. I still thought my son wanted to eat cake. I thought he intended to sit and eat the whole cake right there.

"Don't be silly," I said. "You can't eat a whole cake." By this time, though, he was overtaken by frustration, hunger, and whatever terrible fears had been released as he watched the cake be summarily cut in pieces. When he was offered a slice of cake on a plate, it was not only not what he wanted—it was the very thing he most dreaded being offered. It was a nightmare. It was the head of John the Baptist. He reacted accordingly. Running from the delicatessen toward the information booth, he threw his grieving body onto the hard floor of the terminal. I knelt beside him, trying to comfort him. Sorrow and anger engulfed him. I tried to put my own feelings aside and find a way to help him. There is no helping a tantrum, though; sometimes it just has to run its noisy, awful course. The constellations in the ceiling had seen it all before. An hour later I was able to cajole, bully, and coax him out to Lexington Avenue where we collapsed in a cab.

My son's final tantrum occurred, of course, in the street. We were walking up York Avenue on our way home from a play date when I suggested that we take a shortcut behind an apartment building to get to 81st Street. My son demurred. We took the shortcut. But by the time we were halfway there his protests had escalated to tearful complaints which quickly became loud screams. He was almost five years old by this time, and there was no possibility of just scooping up his wriggling body and carrying him the six blocks to our home. He lay face down on the sidewalk and cried. We had taken the shortcut; he would never be able to go the long way at the precise moment when we took the shortcut. That opportunity was lost forever. It was a cold afternoon, and night was falling. The streetlights were coming on. I tried to drag him along the sidewalk, but this scraped his hands and he began to shriek in between sobs. He was bleeding now. I tried to carry him. He kicked his way free.

People walked by us, smiling in some kind of weird bemusement, or just glad to be on their way somewhere else. I hailed a cab, but after waiting a few minutes with the door opened while I tried to peel my howling son off the pavement, the cab driver took off. I remembered another tantrum I saw once. It was being given by the son of an extremely beautiful and proper Upper East Side matron. The boy, denied something or other, decided to run into the traffic on Madison Avenue to express his frustration. His mother walked ahead of him, trying to ignore his behavior. Every two minutes or so she had to wheel around and grab him, just in time to save him from death under the wheels of the traffic.

My own tantrums are legendary. There was the time I was so upset that the old Wallach's store on Fifth Avenue was shut on Sunday afternoon that my father had to peel my wailing body off the plate glass window. There was even the time a neighbor called the police. After a while, kids don't throw tantrums anymore. There are still tears, there is still agony, but these feelings don't seem to overwhelm and possess the child the way they once did. Maybe the nervous system has matured. Maybe the ability to use language to express feelings takes the pressure off.

Tantrums are so upsetting that it's hard to think clearly about them at the time. It's only now, years later, that I can see the common denominator in all these tantrums. I see that each of my children's tantrums happened after a wish of theirs was ignored by me. In fact these wishes weren't just ignored, they were judged to be inconsequential. (Often they were inconsequential, but that's beside the point.) I had a "don't be silly" attitude about many of these incidents—don't be silly, you can't keep the bathwater in the tub forever; don't be silly, this way is shorter. Being a child is hard because there are so many nos, so many choices made for them without even asking, so many don't be sillys. Children have very little control over many things—what they wear, what they eat, when they come and go. They live with a level of powerlessness that would make many adults explode. They don't have the nervous systems to withstand the onslaught of their frustration. They don't have the tools which keep adults—well, most adults—from screaming and pounding their fists on the floor. Tantrums are their crude, painful way of expressing all this.

It is a strain to remember my children's tantrums. If I hadn't kept a journal, I might have forgotten them completely. I'd like to forget them in a way, and I think that I am meant to forget them. One of the great favors biology does for us is to help us to forget the worst and most difficult parts of raising children. The pain of bearing children is forgotten so fast that there is even a term for it: the amnesia of childbirth. I guess if we could remember what it was like—what the experience of bearing and raising children is really like—we would never do it again. The human race would die out. It's important to forget.

Now when I see an infant, I can hardly imagine how its parents will have the energy, patience, and incredible emotional fortitude to go through what lies ahead of them. Yet, at the time it seemed exhilarating and thrilling and profoundly rewarding. I never regretted it for a second. My children are the best thing in my life and they always have been. They were the most rewarding thing in my life, even when they were having tantrums, even when I was struggling through their illnesses or gritting my teeth or trying not to yell out loud with frustration and fear and anger. Still, I have no idea how I did it, or how anyone does it. That's the forgetting that makes life possible.

DIVORCE

IN THE GRIM MONTHS at the end of my second marriage, I came to think that nothing could be worse for my daughter than to be a prisoner, as she was, in the chilly no-man's-land between our two armies. Her father was on one side of the emotional trench line, and I was on the other. We had talked about separation. We had been to a well-recommended couples counselor. Nothing seemed to diminish our mutual anger and self-righteousness—even our love for our beautiful, enchanting toddler. Her father and I barely spoke beyond the very polite exchange of information which had taken the place of conversation. We had gotten to that terrible place where talking seemed to make everything worse.

I watched my precious, sunny four-year-old grow and learn about the world. Like all mothers I tried to make her wishes come true. Perhaps there was an element of guilt in my machinations. She said she had dreamed that she would get a silver kitten named Moah. One weekend, after an extensive search, we found a silver kitten at a pet store. My husband wrote a substantial check. My daughter delightedly named her real silver kitten Moah. I saw her fall in love with her new kitten and learn to care about her teachers at nursery school.

But I was scared to think what she must be learning about married love. Would she think that love was the dismal emotional disconnection that her parents shared? I was afraid she would somehow be contaminated by our misery, by the bleakness which seemed to have seeped into every corner of our family life. I was afraid that the unhappiness between us was contagious. I decided we should separate, and I told myself that this was as much for our daughter's sake as for ours.

My husband and I would stay friends, of course, and we would be better friends after our separation. We both cared about our daughter. Our separation agreement was drawn up over a steak dinner with our lawyer. Everything would be friendly. I asserted that I didn't want my husband's money. He asserted that he would be happy to pay half of our daughter's expenses. He moved five blocks south and his apartment became her second home. After our separation, he and I had lunch or dinner more often than we had when we were married. We seemed to have become friends again. He picked Liley up every weekend and walked her to school almost every morning. When she missed him, he rushed right over. He and I both explained to her at length that we still loved her dearly. We had just stopped loving each other, that was all.

She didn't accept my explanation. She decided instead that her new kitten had frightened her father away by pouncing on him in bed. Moah was the culprit. She told anyone who would listen—and I was listening very carefully—that her cat had frightened her father. The cat had frightened her father so badly that he had to move away. I knew enough to know that the cat was a stand-in for herself, and I tried to reassure her again and again. Her father loved her, I said. I loved her. The problem was a grown-up problem. For the first time—and certainly not the last—I found myself trying to explain adult insanity to a child.

The kitten made us both laugh as he grew, but nothing could shake my daughter's conviction that she had somehow traded her father for a silver ball of fur. Her dolls, at their tea parties and in the bathtub, began talking a lot about their fathers. Many of them had missing fathers. "My father is in a cage," I heard Barbie explain to Skipper one night. "He's trapped in a cage made of brambles and thorns, brambles and thorns."

Life went on, as it does, and my perfect little plan for my daughter as the treasured child of amicably divorced parents was crushed by its

progress. Within six months of our separation, he flew to the Domini-
can Republic for a divorce. Soon after that he married a woman much
younger than either of us.

Then I remarried. When my daughter was seven, I had another
child, her little brother. Because of my allergies during pregnancy, we
"loaned" her cat to my mother, who lives in the country. I wondered
for a moment if my daughter thought her father might come back once
the cat was gone. She didn't even mention it. Events had overwhelmed
even that childish explanation. My allergies persisted and the cat is still
in the country.

We moved and moved again. Relations between our two households were sometimes less than friendly and sometimes much, much
less than friendly. My daughter's visits with her father slowly diminished, from three days to two, from every weekend to every other
weekend, from a month in the summer to a week in the summer. With
every change, her heart seemed to break.

As a parent who experienced a "good" divorce from my second
husband, and watched my child struggle to deal with it, and then experienced a difficult separation from my third husband and the disintegration of another household, I have many fewer answers than I did
fifteen years ago. The strains of combining two families took their toll;
now we combine three families—and three different last names. I no
longer think that divorce can be a good thing for children. When children are involved divorce is a completely different matter than when
they are not involved. When children are involved in a divorce, they become its innocent victims.

Certainly it's bad for children to live in a household dominated by
parents at war. Certainly it's bad for children to live in the zone of silence
created by adults who have decided they hate each other as much as they
once loved each other. In fact it's not *divorce* that's bad for children, it's
what happens before and after the divorce. If it were possible to separate
and stay amicable, if all parents saw as much of their children after they
remarried as they did just after a divorce, if all stepparents worked out
well, then divorce might be a good thing for children. It isn't.

My separation from my third husband was very different. But
once again a man and I—this time my son's father—explained to a
child that we both loved the child, but that we had just stopped loving

each other. The scenes were dreadfully familiar. I know my daughter
will always be haunted by the loss of her family, just as my son will always mourn the family he imagined and never had. I'll never know
what kind of life my daughter would have had if I had stayed with her
father.

When I ask her about it, Liley, who is a wise, wise teenager now,
reminds me that time doesn't go backward. She reminds me that her little brother is the best thing that has ever happened to her. She says that
she knows her mother and her father will never be together. She says it's
okay. But later I find her curled up in a chair with a book about cats.
She's reading about a breed of hairless cat called a Sphinx. She's looking
for a cat that I won't be allergic to so that we can get another kitten.

THERE'S A BREAKING that happens in a divorce, a shattering of all the
hopes and dreams that both people had once—probably not the same
hopes and dreams, but hopes and dreams nevertheless. Afterward we are
left to live out our lives and our children's lives in the ruins of something we once hoped would be beautiful. We are left with the nightmares and the sadness and the disjointed households and the
stepparents. I know that the wickedness of stepmothers is actually a foil
for the imperfections of mothers. A mother must be ideal, so a stepmother becomes wicked. A father must be a knight in shining armor, so
a stepfather becomes an ogre.

My daughter has had problems with both her stepparents. Both
my children have also had serious problems with any man I have been
involved with. Sometimes, though, a new addition to a family can
change things for the better. At first, my third husband seemed to be a
wonderful stepfather to my daughter. They would go on great expeditions together—although those expeditions were often to a local bar
with fascinating fish tanks. They went shopping together and watched
bad movies on television.

We were traveling, and one night we blundered into a white linen
tablecloth sort of place where every other table seemed to be occupied
by dressed-up families with perfectly behaved children. Dinner was
tense from the moment we sat down in the restaurant: my eight-year-
old daughter, her stepfather, and our baby in a sassy seat. Our hobgob-

lin family, four people just getting to know each other, sometimes seemed as unruly and unpredictable to me as the two dogs we had locked in the car.

Just as we began to eat, my daughter, with one of those clumsy gestures exacerbated by anxiety, knocked her glass of root beer across the table. The fizzy brown liquid spilled over the white linen cloth and napkins and splashed my husband's new shirt before beginning to pool on the polished floor. Everyone in the restaurant turned around to look. As the waiter disapprovingly cleaned up the mess and brought her another drink, I watched my daughter writhe in the hell of public eight-year-old humiliation.

"It's okay," I told her. "Accidents happen." But I could almost hear the voices in her head yelling at her: "Why do you always have to make a mess? How stupid can you be?" Was this the beginning of our new life together? I tried to smile reassuringly, and urged her to try her fresh glass of root beer, but my heart sank.

Then my husband leaned over toward her.

"I'll pay you a dollar to spill that new drink," he said. My daughter looked sharply at him, first in horror, then in confusion, then in wonderment. He was smiling broadly at her. It took me a moment to see what he was up to.

"I'll pay you two dollars not to!" I said.

"Three," my husband said. By now we were all laughing hard. My daughter made ten dollars that night for not spilling her second drink. As we ate and laughed and planned our trip, I tried to imagine my own parents paying me to make a mess. I couldn't exactly, but I did remember many, many times when my parents suggested that the rules—whatever they were at the moment—were much less sacred than my obligation to think for myself. I remember many times when they made me laugh.

It's true that we live in a world where a lot of rules have been shattered. We can't pass on the certainties that were passed on for generations before us. We cannot tell our children that there is a God without preparing them for the doubt that they will find in our world. We can't say that their religion will provide them with tools for living a useful and loving life. We can't promise them that a good education will lead to steady employment. We can't even assure them that the physical world of their childhood—the trees, the seasons, or even the great globe itself—will still be around when they grow up. We can't tell them that marriage is forever.

We expect them to live lives of tremendous regimentation. Many children, including Liley, start school at age two: even their summers are scheduled into day camps and sports camps. Not for them the long unexamined days of my childhood. Their days are measured out in classes, play dates, after-school activities. Structuring their lives makes our lives easier too. We don't spend a lot of time just hanging around with our children these days. This is partly because we have less time. Certainly women of my generation—women who have full-time jobs and are also raising children—have exactly half as much time as the women in our mother's generation. We also have, as endless studies have shown, much less time than men.

I think there's another reason for this too, though. I think we're afraid of our children. They release feelings that are hard to bear, and we are afraid of what would happen if we all went into the kind of free fall that an unstructured weekend sometimes seems to represent. I was certainly afraid of my daughter for years after she was born. I loved her passionately, but I often wasn't sure quite what to do with her. I was willing to play endless games of combing the pastel hair of small plastic ponies or cutting out dolls or dressing and redressing Barbies—but I was immensely bored after only a few minutes. I loved it when she cuddled up next to me. I loved it when we watched a cartoon together or when I read her a book. Watching her sleep peacefully in her crib released the heat of love into my veins.

I wanted to be as perfect for her as my love was; I wanted to be the mother she wanted me to be. I was afraid to reveal the imperfect mother I really was—a mother who might let her daughter watch a sentimental video about the Care Bears for an hour just so that she—the mother—could immerse herself in a bad novel or, worse, a trashy magazine.

One of the things I'm hoping to teach my children is the value of making mistakes. I hope that they will have an understanding of which rules are important and which rules are just convenient. I hope that they will celebrate their failures and mistakes as much as they celebrate their successes. I teach them that the lacy structure of the George

Washington Bridge, a glistening airy silver bracelet, is the way it is be-cause the stone facing didn't arrive—it was a mistake. I want them to remember that Newton discovered the principle of gravity because he was goofing off, and that, as the story goes, the telephone never would have been invented if Alexander Graham Bell hadn't spilled battery acid.

I want them to accept the fact that they will make mistakes. Some-times they will spill their root beer. Sometimes they will be unable to love the people they should love, and they will find it hard not to love the people they should not love. This is nothing more than evidence of their humanity. I want them to glory in their right to be wrong—and to learn from that wrongness. I want them to understand that joke about how Mussolini was the man who made the trains run on time.

It's hard to accept mistakes. Writing about the end of two mar-riages within two decades, I wonder about my own mistakes. There were plenty of extenuating circumstances. My drinking and my third husband's drinking were a huge part of what went wrong. There was infidelity, there was misunderstanding, there were all kinds of bad be-havior. Still, I have two wonderful children who have two different fa-thers—and neither of their fathers lives with us. Both of their fathers have been occasionally very angry at me, and I have returned the favor. Now we are friends. No wonder I hope that my children will learn to celebrate their mistakes; maybe then they can begin to forgive mine.

IT'S NOT THE DIVORCE THAT HURTS

IT STARTED AFTER A VISIT to a toy store around Christmas. "When are you and Dad going to get together? When are you going to get together, Mom?" my son asked. His father and I had been separated for more than five years, but when I heard my son ask this question, I felt as if I had been holding my breath the whole time.

When his father moved out, I hoped my son wouldn't notice. His father had always lived in San Francisco as well as New York. He had often had to pack and leave at a moment's notice. He had often been unable to return when scheduled—even when our marriage was at its strongest. In the last year of our marriage he had rented an office down the street from our apartment where he spent increasing amounts of his time. On the night he left, he had just decided to sleep at his office. It seemed to happen naturally without any of the bitter fighting that characterized the worst parts of our marriage, especially the years when we were both drinking. After dinner he said he was going out and would be back later. I said that when he came in late it woke me up. He said that in order to avoid that perhaps he should sleep in the office. I said fine. The marriage ended not with a bang but with a whimper.

At first my son didn't mention the change in our sleeping arrangements. Our life was still punctuated by his father's departures and arrivals just as it always had been. When his father was in New York he spent hours playing with my son in his room. At night, instead of coming into my bedroom, he walked down the street. By this time, I knew I was a failure at marriage. By this time, I hoped that I might be able to handle divorce in a civilized way.

I sat my son down and explained what had happened. Like millions of separated parents before me, I carefully explained to him that his father and I both still loved him very much, and that we still loved each other, but that we just couldn't live together anymore. I reminded him of our terrible fights. This arrangement would be better, I said. We would still be friends, we would still be my son's parents, but we wouldn't have to fight anymore. I hugged my little boy and cuddled him and assured him that it wasn't his fault. My son took all this in, but he never really asked any questions. So when he calmly turned to me over his macaroni and cheese and asked when his father and I were going to get back together, it released a flood of sadness inside me. I'm a coward; I didn't answer for a while.

As Christmas approached, he asked the question with more and more insistence. "When are you going to get together? Do you think you and Dad could get together?" I didn't really focus on his words. What I heard was the anguish of a little boy whose dearest wish can never come true. I did not listen carefully to what he was saying. Instead of asking myself what he meant, I assumed he meant what I would mean in his circumstances. When I dropped him off at his father's apartment, he grabbed us both by the hands. "When are you two going to get together?" he demanded. His father cleared his throat and looked the other way. I stared at the wall.

"Do you want to have pizza for dinner?" his father said.

Finally, when I saw the dreadful question wasn't going to go away, I settled my son back down on the couch for a talk. He hates talks. His idea of a serious conversation is one that takes place between the front door and the elevator when we're in a hurry. "James," I said, "your father and I are never going to get back together. We both love you very much and we still love each other in a way, but we just can't live together anymore." He stood up and looked down at me as I cowered against the cushions. "Do you mean you are never going to get together?" he demanded.

"It's not your fault," I said.

"Never?"

I took a deep breath. "Your dad and I are never going to get back together," I said.

"Oh no," my son said.

I reached up and stroked his shoulders. "I'm sorry," I said.

"Then I'm never going to get the Neptune Lego Lab!" he wailed, crumpling back down on the couch. It took me a moment to recover.

"The Neptune Lego Lab?"

"You know the one we saw in the store that you said was too expensive!"

Now he was back off the couch and jitterbugging with frustration. "You said it was too much money, but you said if you and Dad got together maybe you could get it for me!"

He was right. He had wanted the Neptune Lego Lab and I had told him it was too expensive. "Maybe if your dad and I get together," I had said, he could get it for Christmas. In questioning me, he hadn't been asking about our divorce, he had been asking about money for a toy. I hadn't been listening to what he was saying. Instead I had been projecting my own feelings onto his innocent question. My son got the Neptune Lego Lab as soon as I could get to the store.

We built the Lego Lab together. I like to think that instead of talking sometimes my son and I build things together. We are excellent at Legos and last summer we built a fabulous tower, taller than either of us with a small motor whose drive shaft moves an assortment of plastic men in an assortment of interesting ways. It took us a week. "Pass me a yellow rod," he would say. "I need a small blue flywheel," I would say. "Let's look at the instructions again." My son thinks we built a hyperspace training tower as the manual instructed us. I think we built a monument to communication.

"People are noticing that the Oedipus story is becoming less and less applicable in our present society," writes the poet Robert Bly in his book *The Sibling Society.* "It doesn't describe current father-son relations. Not only do young men not want to kill their father; many have never even met him." My son has met his father, but he has a father who comes and goes. My son has learned to tell his friends, and himself too, that when his father isn't there when he said he would be—whether it's on my son's birthday or to pick him up after school—it's because "something big" has come up, or because one of his father's friends is in the hospital.

This kind of father has set up a tremendous yearning in my son. He is always afraid to lose his father. He even hesitates to let the man out of his sight for a moment; he never gets enough of his father. It breaks my heart, but I know that's only a fraction of what it does to my son. His father is often apologetic, but nothing changes. "Some spot in the brain that used to hold the substance called responsibility," writes Bly, "now holds the substance called guilt."

The family structure that has been in place for generations of children—for good and evil—has disintegrated before our eyes in the last twenty years. I know this on a sociological and on a personal level. In many ways children have benefited from this change in family structure. Their parents do not rule by divine right. They learn to make their own decisions. They don't end up trapped in a household dominated by his and hers misery and his and hers personal vendettas. I am a much better mother because I'm not forced to live with a man who cheats on me, or a man who hates me, or a man who drinks half a bottle of vodka every day. Still, no one can calculate the loss of an intact family to my children. We have lost a lot. Divorce is a shipwreck, but if we adults behave like adults instead of letting our childish self-righteousness and criticism take over our souls, our children may actually get some benefit along with their heartbreak.

One of the great challenges of life after a divorce is getting along with our ex-husbands and ex-wives, who also happen to be the parents of our children. Somehow, even though we are unable to live with someone, we have to find a way to share with them our most precious assets—our children. In many ways divorce is irrelevant for parents. I will be dealing with my children's fathers for the rest of my life. My dealings with them will be about the things closest to my heart. The things that drove me absolutely crazy when I was living with these men will continue to drive me absolutely crazy when I'm not living with them.

I used to think that people were just behaving irresponsibly when they had children in a marriage they couldn't sustain. Now I think that they are blinded by hope. It doesn't matter, really. The problem is the same. In truth, once two people have had a child, they are bound together for life by that child's existence—whether they want to be or not.

It's part of the perversity of circumstance that couples who can't collaborate in marriage have to collaborate in raising children. Each parent has to stand back—as they couldn't in the marriage—and allow a person they probably don't like or trust very much to have infinite power over the dearest thing in the world—their child. At its most terrible, this problem occurs when one parent suspects that another parent is molesting their child, or endangering the child's physical safety. At its most farcical it's a matter of misplaced clothes and mangled schedules. "Divorce is dumb," says the child of divorce in Erica Jong's book *Megan Has Two Houses*, "because I can never remember where I left my underpants." The heartbreaking part of the book is the little girl's internal adjustment to the situation. "Jeremy is five and I am going to marry him," she says of a playmate. "Then we can have a baby and get divorced. That's what grown-ups do."

Things that seemed irrelevant when I fell in love with my daughter's father are now supremely important. Sharing custody without anger is in many ways harder than staying married without anger. It was hard enough to get along with my ex-husband, a man whom I couldn't manage to live with. Then he remarried. Then I remarried. Suddenly there were four people involved with my daughter's welfare, four people who had to work together and agree on what was right for her.

My son's father sometimes keeps my son out late at night. My son has a great time; I go ballistic. My son's father doesn't think bathing and brushing teeth are very important on the great scale of things. He sends my son to school with black fingernails and spots on his clothes. He sends my son to school with little sleep and unfinished homework. My son doesn't care. I run around after him with clean clothes and a washcloth.

It took a long time for me even to accept responsibility for all this. This isn't a situation that happened to me; this is a situation which I helped create. In a divorce the children are the victims; the parents are the perpetrators. They are the children. We are the adults. This ugly truth is at the basis of helping our children deal with what happens when a family comes apart. I decided to marry these men. I decided to have their children. I decided, or helped decide, that I could no longer live with them. It doesn't really matter what the specific circumstances were—it's always easy to feel the victim. I have to own up to my own decisions.

For me, and ultimately for my son and daughter, the answer has been for me to grow up. Adults take responsibility and they don't waste time on guilt. They don't dream about what didn't happen and what probably won't happen, they act to try and make what is as good as it can be. It was hard for me to behave as an adult no matter what anyone else did. Adults may have hurt feelings, but they don't turn on the person who hurt their feelings. Adults behave politely, no matter what the provocation might be. Adults understand that the answer to someone else's bad behavior is not more bad behavior.

A few years ago, for a story I never wrote, I spent an afternoon in family court watching a judge deliberate on custody cases. Most of the parents I saw were affluent people who had made successes of their lives, but couldn't make successes of their marriages. To my sorrow, I fit that description all too well. What I came away thinking was how many parents—driven by anger—had somehow abdicated their role as parents—educators, supporters, providers of emotional balance and economic security. I don't want to do that. I want to be as much my children's mother as I would be if I were still married to their fathers. I want my children to have the experience of two parents too. If anyone gets caught in the middle, I want it to be the adult who belongs there, not the children who are trying to sort out what has happened to them.

CHILDREN
AND THERAPY

ONE OF THE TALENTS I LEARNED from raising children is the talent of asking for help. Having my daughter overwhelmed me—with passion for her, and with fear about my own abilities to mother her. From the beginning I hired nannies and baby-sitters and anyone I could get to help. By the time my daughter was four, she was in therapy.

As my marriage to Liley's father came apart, in the wake of her birth and my father's death, he and I went into couples therapy with a formidable, very famous woman therapist on the Upper East Side. The psychoanalyst, whom I will call Dr. Dragon, had well-appointed offices with a flame-stitched couch and a pastoral mural with adults dancing around arbors. She was an authoritative woman whose pronouncements were hard to question. When she told us that our four-year-old daughter should be in therapy, we hardly hesitated.

Now, therapy is a complicated matter. There are many therapists—even many pediatric therapists—who start treatment with a prescription. The number of children on Ritalin has skyrocketed in the last few years. Clearly some children do brilliantly on Ritalin and other drugs prescribed to children, but many children don't. Drugs are a tool, a tool that can be used to build a personality or to tear it down, a tool that can enhance character or destroy it. All drugs have side effects. The talking part of therapy is another tool. Like all tools it can be wonderfully effective and terribly destructive, depending on how it is used. The problem is that for therapy to work, real connections have to form between patient and doctor. The patient has to stop believing that the therapy is a tool.

We set up a complicated system with Dr. Dragon and her assistant, whom I'll call Dr. Flowers. Twice a week my daughter went to the therapist's office and "played" for an hour with Dr. Flowers. The office had shelves of toys and books and was a pleasant place where children and therapist sat on the carpet, chatted, drew pictures, and made up stories about a series of dolls and stuffed animals. Then Dr. Flowers reported to Dr. Dragon, who discussed her findings with us, twice a week. This arrangement was as expensive as it was complicated, and as our lives unfolded and Liley's father remarried and I prepared to remarry it became more and more unwieldy. One afternoon, my daughter emerged from the therapist's office covered with small bits of paper with which she had fashioned a skunk costume for herself under the supervision of Dr. Flowers. I was wearing running clothes, and on the way out we ran into Liley's father—double-breasted gray suit, light blue shirt—and her new stepmother—high heels, large straw hat, linen dress.

Dr. Flowers happened to be a loving, funny woman. I called her often for advice, and she gave good advice. I remember one morning in particular. On the occasion of Liley's father's remarriage, I had decided to buy my daughter a puppy. Somehow I thought this might help. The therapist was in favor of this and Liley and I went puppy shopping—an exercise in frustration of course since she fell in love with every puppy we saw. The morning we were scheduled to get the puppy—a few days before the wedding—Liley's father called and said that there could be no puppy. His new wife was allergic to animals, he said.

In a rage, with my daughter weeping in the background, I called Dr. Flowers. She told me not to be angry. She pointed out that my anger would not help my daughter. She suggested that instead of storming down to my ex-husband's apartment to give him a piece of my mind, I go and take him some breakfast and try to talk reasonably. She saved us a dreadful scene that day. My daughter didn't get her puppy then, but later that summer when the whole disagreement had died down, we bought her Lydia—the Welsh corgi who is sulking under my bed as I write.

When I fell in love again, Dr. Flowers also helped me resolve the difficulties with introducing a new man into my family of two. My friends said that my new lover should sleep on the couch. Since he lived in California, he either stayed with me or in a hotel. After a while, the hotels were prohibitive. What would my daughter think when she saw a new man in the bed I had once shared with her father? The therapist gave me a timetable and a series of conversations and explanations for her.

Liley continued in therapy for a while, but somehow—perhaps this was inevitable—the therapist offended her father and he decided that the whole system was wildly expensive and probably damaging. It came to seem to him that, without therapy, we would all be in better shape. Within a few months the therapy was over.

Before a year went by, though, I was looking for another therapist for my daughter. I visited the head of a major therapeutic institution and he told me that my daughter and I—we had stayed very close during our preliminary session—had an unhealthy attachment. I knew that he was right, but that wasn't our primary problem. Then this therapist did the worst thing I think a therapist can do—he implied that if I didn't put my daughter into therapy, preferably psychoanalysis, I would have dire and heartbreaking problems when she was older. She was ten.

It was blackmail, but I fell for it. For two more years I took my daughter to the West Side after school to see yet another therapist. I don't think this woman hurt her, but I'm not sure she helped either. When I called her for advice, she always referred me back to my daughter. After two years, when my daughter's problems didn't seem to be clearing up, when her imagination seemed to be developing to her detriment rather than to her benefit, I began to wonder if the therapy was helping.

It ended one day when Liley and I went canoeing on the lake in New Hampshire where we go every summer. The lake loops around and, at one point, is divided from itself by a narrow strip of land, a line of pines and a dirt road. We decided to paddle the canoe to the other side of this strip and carry it across. It was an experiment in "portage," but it turned out to be a more onerous afternoon than I had imagined. The late afternoon sun was hot, and as we came around the point toward the place where we planned to carry the boat the wind picked up and we had to paddle as hard as we could to keep from being blown backward. The canoe's progress through the water was stopped dozens of feet from the shore. We carried it, wading in deep mud and grass a long way before we were on solid ground. Who knew what worms and creatures lurked in the mud under our bare feet? The canoe got heavier with every step. It was scary, but we made it. More important, we made it laughing.

As we slid the canoe back into the water on the other side, I experienced one of those moments of intense closeness and happiness with my daughter that are part of my life as a mother. We paddled back out into the clear water of the lake, the sandy bottom shimmering beneath us through the water. As the afternoon waned, the sun lay out a watery golden path which seemed to stretch from the mountains in the distance to the faded wood of our dock. "I am so happy," I said out loud. "Me too," my daughter said. Then she thought for a moment. "The doctor says I am permanently scarred," she said. "Do you think I am? Permanently scarred?"

She was wearing a little girl's blue bathing suit and her skin was a velvety tan between its criss-crossed straps. "Permanently scarred?" I said, rolling the idea around in my mind the way I would roll a bad taste around in my mouth before spitting it out. There were a dozen things I wanted to say. Aren't we all permanently scarred? Isn't life about making those scars beautiful and useful rather than dwelling on them? Of all the phrases in the world, what could apply less to my innocent, gorgeous daughter laughing in the sunlight than "permanently scarred"? Instead I said, "What do you think she meant?" But my daughter had already lost interest.

"Mom! we're almost there," she said excitedly. "Look, Lydia's waiting for us on the dock." She was right, in the distance I could see the anxious form of my daughter's dog peering out over the water at the spot where we had disappeared around the point hours before. I decided to be happy. I decided to let Liley be happy if she could. I decided that life is infinitely more mysterious than the formulas that therapy applies. After a few more sessions, I cut back to once a week, and when Christmas vacation came Liley stopped altogether.

So it was with mixed feelings and a great deal of confusion that, a few years later, I listened to my son's teacher suggest therapy for my son. The situation was complicated and distressing. Because my son's father always divided his time between New York and California, my son's passionate bond with him was always being interrupted by his necessary trips away. This drove me crazy and it made my son very sad.

By the time my son was in second grade his father and I had separated, and his trips to California had become longer and even less predictable. About the time that this stopped bothering me, it began to weigh my son down more and more. Soon his father's long absences seemed to become almost unbearable. His father would leave and he would be all right for about two weeks. Then he would begin to feel sad. This sadness became like a tangible object. It seeped into many things my son did; it kept him from enjoying himself. Most of all, it distracted him at school so that instead of listening or doing schoolwork, he was overtaken by longing. Being with his father is always my son's goal, as if a part of his heart can't rest unless he is with this man who makes his heart so restless.

So when my son's pediatrician and his teacher suggested therapy, I thought long and hard. I remembered my daughter's therapy and my own therapy, which began when I was about twelve. Every Wednesday afternoon after school my mother drove me to White Plains. The therapist smoked a pipe and sat behind a desk. He told me stories about his other patients. I liked the story about the man who had tried to kill him with the office chair. I knew I was supposed to tell stories too, but I mostly made them up. The whole thing was an exercise in something, but that something wasn't about me. The therapist called a meeting with my parents. He told my parents I was brilliant. "She has a Cadillac engine in there," he said. My father loved to tell this story.

So I decided not to send my son to a psychiatrist. Instead I went back to one myself. I have serious doubts about a child's ability to absorb the benefits of therapy. Children sometimes feel stigmatized by being in therapy and this doesn't make it easier for them. I went back to the couples therapist who had treated me and my son's father. It worked. This man, who knew the situation, was able to advise me about how to handle my son. He gave me a reading list. He encouraged and reassured me. Buttressed by his encouragement, I coaxed my son into talking. I never, ever interrupted him. I never criticized the man he was talking about. I suggested that my son's sadness was natural and completely understandable. I also suggested that he try to find a way to keep that sadness out of school—a place where he needed to pay attention. The sadness passed. The second grade resumed. That was three years ago.

SCHOOL

"IS IT A SCHOOL DAY?" my son asks when his eyes open in the morning.

"Yes," I say, and then I try to sugarcoat this unwelcome information. "But it's a short day," I'll say. Or, "But you have a play date with Luca," or, "After school we're going swimming!" or, "It's Friday!"

He staggers into my bedroom and falls back on the big bed, groaning with his hand to his forehead. Still in his dinosaur pajamas he curls up into a ball to indicate abdominal pain. "I feel so sick!" he says. His adorable body goes limp, his eyes roll back in his head, his bare feet dangle over the edge of the covers.

"You feel sick?" I try to keep my voice serious, but something about my son in his pajamas just makes me want to laugh with delight and shout with joy. His brown hair is sticking up in three directions. One ear is still red from being pressed against the pillow. His pajama tops are rolled up to reveal a strip of smooth skin. One hand is half blue from an experiment with a marker and some olive oil just before bedtime. This is one of those moments when I can't believe my luck. I didn't do anything to deserve this wonderful child; his existence on my bed is evidence of God's grace.

"I'm sick," he says, now leaning back against the pillows. "I think I have a fever." That's the rule in our household. If you have a fever you go to the doctor; if you don't have a fever, you go to school. Of course sometimes I call the doctor and he doesn't need to see my son and then there's a delicious day in bed with treats and relaxing movies and cartoons and the other perks of illness. I reach over to feel his forehead. It's cool and soft. "I'm too sick to go to school," he concludes, trying to make his little-boy voice sound big and definite.

His voice has already been drowned out by the Good Mother Committee in my head. He's just a little boy, the committee says. Show him that it's all right to be lighthearted. He'll only be this cute for a moment; go ahead and curl up with him and read him the story about the elephant's child. He'll probably learn more that way anyway. Then the Bad Mother Committee chimes in reminding me that letting him skip school is teaching him to be irresponsible. If he misses school today, he's just learning to lie and he'll probably grow up to be a serial killer and it will be because of this day, this Tuesday in May, the day I didn't make him go to school. "Didn't he miss a lot of school as a young child?" I can hear the psychologists asking.

"You have to go to school," I say. "You like school."

"I don't like school, I hate school," my son says, pulling the covers up to his adorable chin and flashing his dimpled smile at me. "It's boring. I'd rather stay home with you."

I hated school too. This didn't bother my parents, who were parents of the go-to-school-no-matter-what school. They would haul me out of bed. "I'm dead," I would explain, crumpling into a heap on the floor. They would dress me and prop me up at the breakfast table. If I was still dead when it was time to leave, my father would half drag, half carry me into the elevator and then half drag, half carry me to school. "She's dead," he would explain to the teacher as I slumped in the doorway of the classroom. "Again?" the teacher would ask.

"I'm sorry you don't like school," I say to my son, "but you have to go anyway." I'm weakening, but I struggle to keep my voice convincing.

"But I don't want to go!" he protests. Tears well up in his eyes, but he's smiling.

"Children have to go to school just the way grown-ups have to go to work," I say, but as far as I'm concerned he's won. I'm already planning our day.

"Well, if I go can I have a play date with Luca?" he asks.

"No problem," I say.

. . .

WHETHER OR NOT a particular child should go to school on any particular given day is hard enough to decide: school takes up a huge part of our children's lives and is one of the principal influences we provide for them. In *The Nurture Assumption,* Judith Harris has written convincingly that peers are more important in children's development than parents. "Do parents have any important long-term effects on the development of their child's personality? This . . . examines the evidence and concludes that the answer is no," she writes. If so, the principal influence on children's personality is surely the heart of their community—their school. But it is we parents who decide where and how children will be educated. This decision is one of the hardest we have to make as parents.

For many years, the first issue of parenting is this: where should your child go to school, and what should your relationship be to that school? Parents choose their children's schools for dozens of reasons. Obviously a school should be chosen with the child in mind. If a child is unhappy at school, parents should listen to the child. Listening is a powerful act. Although, in our overexcited world, listening can seem passive, it's the most important activity a parent can cultivate. This is especially true when it comes to a child's experience in school. School is a world where parents can't follow; the child's testimony is often the only evidence a parent has about what happens there.

Even as early as nursery school, my own educational career was disastrous. By fifth grade I was the class scapegoat. Where school was concerned, I began to come unglued. "Kids feel a sense of purposefulness when they are rooted in a world that makes sense," says James Garbarino in *Lost Boys: Why Our Sons Turn Violent and How We Can Save Them.* "It makes sense to follow the rules if you feel the authority that makes the rules has your interests at heart. It makes sense to respect your elders if you see them as powerful, well-intentioned, in charge of the world in which you live, and benevolent toward you." Finally as a senior I found a school I liked. I became a teacher after college to try and preach the ideas of that school. I did not want my own experience at school to influence what happened to my children.

I chose my daughter's first school because it was in the same build-

ing as the church I went to. I chose my son's first school because it was
the closest nursery school to our apartment. The school my daughter
attended was private, and it was wonderful for her for a few years. She
was lucky. She had good teachers. It was an odd hybrid of a school, a
cross between the old alternative schools and the pressured schedules of
New York's Upper East Side.

By the sixth grade, though, this school had become a kind of hell
for my daughter. A smart, verbally quick, overweight beauty, she was
teased and harassed by both students and teachers. She shared a building
with a high school population who thought nothing of making lewd
and cruel comments about her developing body. When she complained, I listened. Often, though, it seemed as if there wasn't much I
could do. I protested again and again to her teachers. I called the head
of the school at least once a week. At first my daughter wouldn't tell me
the names of her tormentors. Even when she did, they were only mildly
reprimanded. The worst of the boys was, however, threatened with sus-
pension and he stopped speaking to my daughter. Others replaced him.
We live in a world where people are always railing against injustice. I
couldn't bear to have my daughter find out that when justice collides
with self-interest, self-interest often wins.

At the end of sixth grade, she expressed a desire to go to an all-girls
school and I immediately sent for applications. At one school she was
told by a woman who hadn't even bothered to introduce herself that
her math scores were too low for the school. "We require excellence,"
this woman said. At another school when my daughter said she had organized her classmates to protest sexist stereotypes among mice in a
children's book titled *Abel's Island,* the head of the school was horrified.
"Is that some kind of women's lib thing?" she asked. Finally, although
we are not Catholic, Liley ended up at a private Catholic girls school, a
school as it turned out that had the confidence and the intelligence to
educate her emotionally and intellectually at the same time.

My son went to a private nursery school, and most of his classmates went on to private school. It took me a long time to translate my
doubts about private school into the courage to consider public school.
Public school in New York City—if you read the newspapers—sounds
like a cross between a prison and a war zone. In the days before my son's
first day of kindergarten, I read story after story about the collapse of

the public school system. The chancellor quit. The mayor cut the school budget by another gazillion dollars. Stories profiled school administrators saying they weren't sure if they would have the budget to hire any teachers at all. The local paper ran a story on one class that—for lack of space—met in a broken shower stall. There were hearings on students using box cutters as weapons in the public schools.

About a week before my son started school, the principal asked each parent to write a letter introducing their child to their new teacher. That sounded okay. I took to walking by the school regularly to see if I noticed weapon-wielding ten-year-olds or plaster falling into the street. Sometimes there is peeling paint in my son's school, but the only weapons wielded in there are the weapons of curiosity and the love of learning. My son is learning the basics my daughter missed, and his reluctance to go to school is usually as pro forma as it was on that morning in May.

I don't know if there's an answer to the question of how best to educate our kids, except that like many things it's a patchwork of what's available to any given family. I do know that my own experience of school—as a student and later as a teacher—is irrelevant to my children's experience, and I think that has helped them. When it comes to choosing schools, I would say that the most important thing to look for is mood. It's hard to measure moods, but a good school is staffed by adults who generate good feelings. They know that their work is effective. They respect one another. They have clear ideas of what is acceptable and what is not acceptable, and they are able to deal with crises in a calm way. They smile often, and yell infrequently.

"WHAT IS THE DIFFERENCE between the approach of our grandparents and ourselves in disciplining children?" asks Haim Ginott in *Between Parent and Child*. "Whatever grandfather did was done with authority; whatever we do is done with hesitation. Even when in error, grandfather acted with certainty. Even when in the right, we act with doubt." Ginott's description is a reaction to modern uncertainty and the permissiveness of our generation of parents—a permissiveness which often encourages children to tyrannize us. Still, there is nothing good about acting with certainty when you are wrong. Parents are often wrong.

The trick is to approach our errors without guilt and with humor—not to pretend that they don't exist.

When I was younger, I swore that my children, if I had children, would never have violent toys or ugly plastic stuff or watch stupid cartoons on television—if they watched television at all. God must have been laughing. I write this on a computer which is also equipped with war games, and a Lego warrior complete with nuclear arsenal competes for space on my desk. The tables and shelves in my son's room are already packed with Lego rockets and spaceships and cannons which he assembles while watching cartoons where Elmer Fudd tries to annihilate Bugs Bunny with a shotgun or where Megatron zaps Cheetor with his death ray.

When I was growing up my brothers and I didn't have violent toys and we didn't have television. Instead we acted out with each other. I thought my job was to cause my brother pain; he thought his job was to complain and get me into trouble with our parents. This was an uglier kind of violence than Beastwars or Elmer and Bugs. My idea of fun was appearing in Ben's room with a spoonful of sugar and a dish of salt and watching him spit and gag as he realized that with me what you saw was not often what you got. When we were older Ben and I turned on our younger brother, Fred, initiating him into our sadistic sibling society with some serious hazing. At one point he had to wade into a lake in his beloved new cowboy boots. I remember with terrible regret the way he sobbed as his boots filled with the slimy water.

My children don't act that way. They play at being violent, but they don't abuse each other or their friends. They squabble, but their real power is never brought into play. Both my kids are trusting and sweet with their friends. My son is one of the biggest kids in his class but he never uses that strength to hurt another child. I know a little bit about violence. Twenty years ago I was attacked by a stranger, and after that I bought myself a pistol and learned how to use it. I don't believe that toy weapons are the same as real weapons, or that violent cartoons create violent people. Real violence is not the drama of Elmer Fudd or Sylvester and Tweety, or the Power Rangers or even the video games with their frightening titles: Turok, Body Harvest, Maximum Carnage. Real violence is the abuse of the power of one person or group of people over another. Real violence is as intimate as it is impersonal. It doesn't happen on stage or on television, it happens in our living rooms and bedrooms and the streets where we live.

"WHAT'S A STEALTH BOMBER?" my son asks.

I show him a newspaper with a map of the most recent war and the bombing sites hit by NATO planes. "It's an airplane which is used to drop bombs when a country is at war," I say. "It's terrible." I don't watch television news with my kids around, but it's impossible to avoid images of rows of corpses and fleeing refugee families on the newsstand.

"Why do they call it a stealth bomber?"

"It's designed to avoid being detected by radar," I say, uncomfortably.

"Cool!" my son says. "The Nighthawk, look at this!" He turns the page to a photo of the newest bomber.

"Look at that laser coating," my son says. "Wow! There are the bombs. The radar can only pick it up when they drop a bomb. That's awesome!"

"Bombs are not cool," I say. "They destroy everything they hit. They destroy innocent people."

"They destroy innocent children and all their toys," my daughter adds, big-sister style.

"Okay, what they do isn't cool, but bombs are cool, explosions are cool. Look there's an aircraft carrier. Which of these planes come from the carrier? Are they using any ground troops?" I try to insulate my children from violence, but my son is fascinated. A friend of mine who refused to buy her sons toy guns gave in when they started nibbling their graham crackers into the shapes of guns at snack time and staging a full-scale war.

"Listen," I say. "It is not all right for people to kill each other. It is not awesome in any way. It is not all right for people to drive each other away from where they live, and it's not all right for our country to be bombing people who have never attacked them."

"Okay, okay, Mom." My son is reading the captions under the photographs of the stealth bomber.

"War is wrong," I say, feeling righteous and definite.

"Wasn't your father a soldier?" my daughter asks. My kids have seen photographs of my father, proudly wearing his World War II uniform. They have visited my father's grave and noticed the veteran's flag that waves there.

"That was different." I hate these arguments that end in sticky ambiguity. Perhaps I'm a bleeding-heart liberal. I'm certainly glad we won World War II. Still, I've always had a hard time with the argument that you can prevent some bad suffering by causing some good suffering.

Later the same day the kids and I went to the supermarket to fill brown bags for a local food pantry. There is plenty of suffering just a few blocks away from where we live. I fill my shopping bag with powdered milk and foods high in nutritional value. My son fills his with peanut butter and macaroni and cheese. When it comes to helping other people, he has better instincts than I do. He wants other children—poor or not—to have what he has. I want to share my extra money; he wants to share his life. As we leave the supermarket, my son's eagle eye is caught by photographs of Apache helicopters. "Killer choppers," he mutters excitedly under his breath. "Those are the ones with the missiles!"

INVENTING
ADOLESCENCE

ONE OF MY WORST MEMORIES as a mother is from almost eight years ago. It was a hot day and as I was struggling home from the market with the baby in a backpack, a shrieking eight-year-old threatening to run into traffic, and the family's recalcitrant dog on a fraying leash, I ran into an old friend and her teenage daughter. We were loaded down with bulging plastic bags of cereal, milk, and kibble from Sloans; they had slim glossy shopping bags from Searle and Talbots.

The woman had been my friend when we were both young and had money to spend on clothes. Now I felt haggard, and she was a beautiful woman of a certain age. We were in full cry; the baby whining, my daughter begging and tugging, the dog pulling, and me trying to control with my voice a group which might have been better controlled by an infantry platoon.

To me it looked as if my friend and her daughter, in their nifty suits, walking down the street in laughing conversation as their blond hair gleamed in the sun, were the epitome of glamour and cool. I reached up with my unmanicured hand and let it rest on my friend's cashmere shoulder, a shoulder unspotted by tears or spit-up. I wanted just to hold on to another adult for a moment. Suddenly the dog lunged forward, tipping me off balance, and the baby banged into my head. He started to cry. It was all I could do to keep from crying myself.

My friend smiled seraphically as she sized up my situation. "It's not so bad," she said, stepping away. "Wait until you have a teenage daughter."

I smiled, but I was furious. Wait? I thought. This isn't bad enough? Perhaps she has forgotten what it's like to have small children, or perhaps she had a nanny to do all the tough stuff, two nannies, three nannies. Wait? Easy for her to say as she strolls back from Madison Avenue after an afternoon of civilized shopping and conversation. Easy for her to say!

Now I have a teenage daughter.

And it's true, my daughter doesn't whine and shriek, and she doesn't require physical care and feeding every four hours. She is infinitely capable of taking care of her own physical needs. But being the mother of a teenage daughter is the kind of hard that makes herding and feeding cranky children seem easy. It's the kind of hard I hate the most. It's the kind of hard that requires actual change in me. In order to be a good mother for my almost grown-up daughter, I am being forced to be completely grown-up myself.

My daughter has been a teenager for five years now. In her characteristic teenage mannerisms—her worries about what her peers will think of her, her obsession with the shifting friendships in her class, her fears about looks and clothes, her instinct to defy for defiance sake, her rebellion against any rules or conditions which might be less than fair for her or anyone else—I recognize another teenager I have lived with a long time—myself. For four decades now, more or less, I have been weighing myself in the morning and letting the number on the scale determine my mood. For all that time I have been looking at myself in mirrors and letting the way I look dictate the way I feel.

I've had half a lifetime of walking into parties and wondering whether the evening would be a success, based on my estimate of how many people liked me. I'm a middle-aged woman in jeans and T-shirts; my favorite is a blue one that says "Irreverence Justified" in bright pink script. I have perennially blond hair and I'm surprised when the twenty-year-old on the next treadmill turns up the speed to where I can't go.

I don't like having to grow up, but my daughter helps me. "Are you going to take a shower?" I'll ask her when what I really mean is that her hair is dirty.

"Don't be so critical," she groans, sighing deeply as if she were the adult and I the difficult child.

For a moment I forget our family adage, that when you argue with a toddler, or with a teenager, you have already lost. "I'm not always critical," I say. "I'm very positive about your looks." I tell my daughter often how great her hair looks and how beautiful she is. I also tell her that she has beautiful, almond-shaped blue eyes and that her skin glows like porcelain.

"Yeah, Mom," she says, bored now because she has already won and she can't quite summon up the energy to finish me off. "But it's always about my looks."

Bingo. My generation has resisted the physical encroachments of age as if it was a terrible enemy which could somehow be defeated if we were smart enough or rich enough or had enough time. "Modern parents' reaction to their children's coming into the flower of youth at a time when the parents are about to begin their decline is more often to deny that this is so by trying to remain as beautiful, as young, as strong, and as attractive as the child," says Bruno Bettelheim disapprovingly in *A Good Enough Parent*. But we have refused to give in to age for a good reason—there is no such thing as a gracefully aging American woman. Either you're a babe, or you're invisible. Between miniskirts from the Gap and streaky blond hair and shapeless flowered dresses and gray hair there is . . . nothing.

I can rationalize this all I want, but when my daughter became a teenager I had to move over. I had to stop behaving as if I were eighteen. I had to let go of how I looked and what people might think of me. It's my daughter's turn. It's her turn to worry about other people and wear T-shirts with smart messages and question everything everyone says. It's her turn to be ruled by clothing fads and weep over what grades she gets and spend hours talking about which friend did this or that to this or that friend and what that might mean.

When I began to change in order to accommodate my teenage daughter, my life relaxed a lot. I stopped reading women's magazines—which are all directed at teenagers and illustrated with photographs of teenagers—and got a subscription to a news magazine. I stopped spending hours analyzing other people's behavior. What I don't know now, I'm probably not going to learn. I had to invent a new personality for myself, a personality which would allow my daughter to have the mirror, borrow my best clothes because they look better on her, and monopolize all conversations about the behavior of young females. I had to give up the idea that I would ever be the teenager I never got to be. Somehow, against all odds, I still had a dream that I might metamorphose backward in time to become the perfect nymphet of my own dreams. It sounds absurd, but our fantasies often are absurd. I had to let go of that dream and embrace the idea that I might be a fabulous middle-aged woman and a great mom.

CHILDHOOD ITSELF is a recent invention, as Philippe Ariès has brilliantly shown in his book published in 1961, *Centuries of Childhood*. "In the tenth century, artists were unable to depict a child except as a man on a smaller scale," he points out. Ariès argues that Wagner's *Siegfried* was the first modern adolescent. "The music . . . expressed for the first time that combination of (provisional) purity, physical strength, naturism, spontaneity and joie de vivre which was to make the adolescent the hero of our twentieth century." In the scant forty years since Ariès wrote, the adolescent hero has become a kind of villain in the American family drama. These days almost all parents of teenagers seem united in their common ritual of complaint. "I have a teenager," and especially, "I have a teenage daughter" are phrases usually accompanied by a rolling of the eyes and grunts of assent. "I guess I have a few good years left before it happens," the mother of a ten-year-old girl said to me last week.

"It doesn't have to happen," I said. "My teenager and I are still good friends." Across the lawn our children were playing volleyball.

"There's all this research," she said. "They all say that girls are at risk during the years from thirteen to seventeen." The volleyball game had degenerated into a game of freeze tag.

"That doesn't mean we have to turn on them," I said.

Today's newspaper has a story about four teenagers who disappeared from their suburban homes and spent four days in New York City without bothering to tell their parents where they were. "You can't get inside the mind of a teenager," one of the fathers explained to the reporter who wrote the story. That seemed to be a sufficient explanation for the disappearance of his child. Of course you can't get inside the mind of anyone else, no matter what age they are. Somehow our teenagers have become the designated hitters in our families. Our teenagers have taken on—or been given—the job of acting out all our anger and getting blamed for it as well.

Teenagedness as we know it is truly modern. It's true that adolescence is a time of tremendous physical changes. It's a time when children become physical adults with all that implies. What's different is the way society defines and reacts to those changes. There are no teens in ancient history or in the Greek myths. There are no teens in the great novels of the nineteenth century. Through most of history the transformation of a child to an adult has happened in a day or a moment. Spiritually that moment was a first communion or a bar mitzvah. Socially that moment came when a girl pinned up her hair, put on a gown, and made her debut. For men it was often a rite of passage performed among other men. It was the moment when a child became a man and when a girl became a woman.

Sometime in the last hundred years, this pivotal moment began extending like our culture's reflection in a fun-house mirror. Mark Twain invented characters whose teenagedness became part of their story. Then J. D. Salinger wrote the ultimate teenage novel, *The Catcher in the Rye.* These days the moment of passage from childhood to adulthood has grown even longer so that the teen years—with their youthful looks, unbridled freedom, lust for experimentation, and righteous urges—seem to intrude further and further into what used to be called adulthood. These days, it sometimes seems, many successful people are lifetime teenagers. Like Ted Turner and Jane Fonda, or the adults who go on expensive adventure trips, or grown-ups who buy the sports cars and electronic devices that they refer to as "toys." What was once a moment, and quite recently became a decade, now stretches into old age.

And what will become of the real teenagers—those children who are actually in their teen years—whose parents are still older versions of themselves? How can a child rebel against a parent who is still rebelling? How can a child experiment if the child is part of a parent's experiment to begin with? Recently a friend asked me for advice about her teenage daughter. The problem for our generation, she told me, was how to tell our children not to do things which we were still doing.

How could she tell her daughter to stop smoking pot, she asked, when she herself still frequently smoked pot? How could she tell her daughter not to drink too much when her daughter occasionally saw her under the influence?

ONE NIGHT, when I was about fourteen, my father—who had quite a few martinis by that hour of the evening—decided it was time to tell me about sex. He told me in graphic, passionless detail while I squirmed with embarrassment. From his description, I assumed that sex was dirty, and that the sex act was shameful and that it should be done only in the bathroom.

"Do you need to know anything about sex?" I ask my daughter one evening as we're walking down 86th Street. Crowds of people are streaming out of the subway on the way home from work. Sidewalk vendors hawk bestsellers and incense, fresh fruit and candied nuts. The smell of burnt sugar follows past store windows filled with shoes, clothes, party hats, cameras, and books. There are lots of distractions. I don't want her to feel trapped. I feel trapped.

"I know enough already," she says. Then in a singsong voice she adds, "It's the way we populate the planet."

"How do you know that?" I ask.

"From coed sex education class, we learned all about it in sixth grade," she says.

"What about birth control?"

"Mom, we spent a whole year on that! We learned how to put a condom on a banana!" I wince. She makes sex sound like just another subject, not quite as interesting as English but a little less boring than algebra. "Anyway it doesn't matter," my daughter says. "You know I hate men."

"You don't hate all men," I say.

"No," she says. "Just the ones I know." I want to argue with her but we're home now, crossing the lobby toward the elevators. I remember the years when I had just become a teenager, the years of my first tight skirts and high heels, and the years when I thought the embodiment of male perfection was the great Elvis Presley. I was a slow learner when it came to sex. I was nineteen before any man even really kissed me.

When I finally did sleep with a man, it meant something. It meant so much in fact that I thought we should get married—an illusion fortunately not shared by the man in question. I didn't hate men, but I was pretty sure they hated me.

When I ask my writing students about how children should be taught about sex, they surprise me with many different answers. One woman was brought up in a house where sex was openly discussed and nudity was the norm; she says this helped her understand and appreciate her own adult sexuality. Another woman says she has never allowed her children to ask about the sex she has with her husband; this has taught them to respect adult privacy. A third says that no one in her house ever discussed sex specifically, but that her mother brought her up to investigate everything she did before she did it; as a result her first sexual experiences were positive, because she was prepared.

It's a different world now. When I was a teenager, twenty-one-year-olds were grown-ups, men and women looking forward to having families, settling down and getting jobs they hated, so that they could save up for a retirement when it was all over. Sex was only for married people. Only young women who were engaged were eligible for birth control. In those days the fear of pregnancy kept us in line, but these days there is much more to fear. My daughter lives in a world where any sixth grader knows more than I did on my wedding night.

Baby-sitters

I GREW UP in the prosperous postwar suburbs of New York City, and when I turned twelve, I noticed my parents' friends beginning to eye me in a special way and chat me up at cocktail parties. Later, I heard through my bedroom walls as they asked my parents: "Do you think Susie would like to baby-sit sometime?" I loved baby-sitting. Playing with other people's children was sometimes trying, but being in their houses and seeing how they lived was fascinating. I loved the power of being—temporarily—the head of the household, delegated to give orders about bath time and bedtime.

It was after bedtime that the job really came to life. I browsed through these strange family's medicine cabinets, ogled their family photographs, flipped through the unpaid bills on their desk, inspected their cabinets and refrigerators, scanned the books on their shelves, and mentally recorded their family traditions and habits—habits which were fascinating and exotic because they were so unfamiliar. I knew which married couples slept in single beds. I knew who was reading *The Joy of Sex,* and which pages they had bookmarked. I knew which Daddy kept photo magazines featuring artistic nudes in his tie drawer. I never found lewd Polaroids, or love letters, or piles of hundred dollar bills in an underwear drawer—but for me there was delight in knowing about the texture of other people's lives. I was fascinated by the secrets of the adult world. The combination of this private knowledge and the power of being the responsible person in a sleeping house was a heady mixture for a thirteen-year-old.

When the parents came home, I was always demurely sitting in the living room reading *Anne of Green Gables* or *Young Renny* by Mazo de la Roche—the kinds of novels I kept on hand for this purpose. Without knowing it, I understood that I was one-dimensional for the people I worked for. They had no idea that I might have thoughts and feelings that were hidden from them—including irritation at their children. They never imagined that I had a life of my own or an intense curiosity about their lives. They didn't wonder, or didn't want to wonder, about what happened when they were gone. I was the baby-sitter and as long as I behaved in a conventional baby-sitter way while they were around, they would never imagine anything different.

"Yes, Mrs. Esterhazy," I would say, "the children went to bed on time."

"Thank you Mr. Esterhazy," I would say as the man of the house slipped me a few five dollar bills and I inhaled the smoky, whiskey smell of adults after parties. "I'd love to baby-sit for you again, anytime."

WHEN I NEEDED to hire a baby-sitter myself, twenty-five years later, I forgot all about my own experiences as a baby-sitter. As soon as I was pregnant, I began to wonder how to get the help I needed in taking care of my baby. I felt completely inadequate to take care of anything myself. I was living in Manhattan, and I called the most expensive agency. They sent an elderly Irish woman named Mrs. Moan to interview us in our small apartment. Then the agency called and said Mrs. Moan didn't want to work for us. We were off to a bad start in finding a baby-sitter, and I had no idea of the incredible difficulties, heartbreaks, anger, and expense that we would all live through before both my children were in school all day.

Finding a baby-sitter is one of the greatest challenges facing women of our generation, women who have to juggle real jobs and real domestic responsibilities. I have a friend who admitted to me that she didn't have a third child because finding a baby-sitter had been such a dreadful problem. Most of the baby-sitters available in New York City during the time I have had children are young women from Jamaica, other islands in the Caribbean, or the Philippines who have come to New York in search of economic opportunity. Many of them have left their own children and families behind—children and families who are counting on their earnings for support. Many of them are illegal aliens—in all my searching for baby-sitters in New York, I succeeded in finding only two legal candidates, and they were legal because they had each paid between $5,000 and $10,000 to marry an American man they hardly knew.

Selecting a baby-sitter from this pool of deeply ambivalent women, whose opportunity for envy and resentment are more than ready-made, is very difficult. On top of that there is the difficulty of being a mother who has to turn over the care of her precious, precious children to a virtual stranger in order to go to work—work which is often necessary to provide for the children. One of the great myths of our time is that women "choose" to go to work; most women have no choice. (Of course many of the baby-sitters have already gone through the same thing. They also have few choices.) It's no wonder that the arrangement between these two groups of women is difficult at best and tragic at worst.

Of course I didn't realize any of this when I hired Juana. Juana was a reserved woman, and although she talked like a political refugee, in fact she and her family had moved to Queens from her home country to make a better life for themselves. Juana had worked as a baby-sitter and cleaning lady for a woman I knew and admired for her flamboyant, spirited good looks. This woman wanted someone who would live in. She offered me Juana with glowing recommendations. I was too anxious already to worry much about anyone's motivations. Juana came to work for me as a cleaning lady for a few months before I had my daughter, and she stayed on as a full-time nanny for almost six years, traveling to New Hampshire with us in the summer and showing up five or six days a week and staying until midnight when we asked her to.

She seemed to care about my daughter, but when her son joined us I was shocked to see how much more she cared about him. That's how blind I was to her real feelings. Juana was as one-dimensional for me as I had been for those parents for whom I was the baby-sitter. I didn't—couldn't—remember what it had been like to be a baby-sitter myself. Leaving my daughter with Juana, even in the safety of our apartment, to go to my office and work on a book was one of the most painful things I have ever done. I was writing a book about my father, who had just died, and I often felt I was being asked to choose between honoring the dead and caring for the living.

In the morning, after Juana came, I would walk across the park to the room where I worked at writing, feeling physically as if a string tied to my heart and gut was being jerkily paid out over the grid of Manhattan streets. I called all the time; the line was often busy. This made me furious. In fact, I was often in a rage at Juana. Juana made a mess in the kitchen, and Juana sometimes dressed my baby in clothes she knew I hated. On the one hand I didn't trust Juana at all—why should I? I didn't know her. I had never been to her house in Jackson Heights; she had never invited me. I didn't let her take my daughter out of our apartment for the first year of her life. On the other hand, I was forced to trust Juana with the care of the only thing that meant anything to me. It took me years to see that my feelings about Juana had nothing to do with Juana at all. They were feelings provoked by being in an impossible situation.

When we went to New Hampshire, and Juana brought along her son and her mother, I got a clearer look at how different we were. Our lake in New Hampshire is crystal clear and protected by various private and state agencies. Juana's mother thought it looked like a good place to do the laundry. It was cold in New Hampshire, but instead of turning on the heat, Juana built a fire. Once, in New Hampshire we were driving, and a rusted-out old truck driven by a weathered old farmer cut us off. "He's just an old *campesino,*" I said with contempt. *"Mi padre es un campesino,"* Juana said.

When my marriage to my daughter's father ended, though, something in our tenuous relationship shifted. Juana said she needed the summer off. Her husband wanted her to go to Mexico. I patiently explained to her why that was impossible. I had sponsored Juana for her green card and she had already taken three weeks off. I felt as if she owed me. I guess she felt the same way. She was sick, she said, and she had to take time off to recover. She told me she went to her doctor and that she had heart problems. I had insisted that she see my doctor—a real doctor. I was as blind to my own arrogance as I was to Juana's heart.

She missed two appointments. She said she couldn't find his office. When he finally examined her he told me there was nothing wrong with her. "She just wants to take a vacation," he said.

The Sunday after that, Juana quit, leaving my keys and a note with the doorman. I was angrier than ever, but it didn't do me any good. Later that year Juana came back from her vacation and went to work for a friend of mine. I asked if she would come and visit; I thought that might help my daughter to know that the woman who was her best friend hadn't just disappeared. She didn't come; I never saw her again. Looking back, I can see my own obtuseness, but I can also imagine my daughter's grief when the woman who had been a constant in her life since infancy just vanished one day.

By this time, my daughter was in school and I decided I needed someone who was more of a tutor than a baby-sitter. I hired Cara, a cultured woman who had been a teacher in her home country. I paid her exactly twice what I had paid Juana. After Cara had been working for me for a while, I learned—slowly—that she had left six children behind in the countryside with no adult. The oldest child was fourteen, and they were completely dependent on the money she sent home and on her monthly phone calls. Juana had been calm and reserved. Cara was warm and outgoing and brilliant at keeping the house in order. When I hired Cara, I hired someone else to clean the apartment. Cara was too good, I hoped, for housecleaning. When the cleaning lady left, though, Cara asked for her job. I relented. By that time I understood that Cara's heart was far away and half broken by her own situation.

Later, I had another child and I hired another baby-sitter to supplement Cara. That baby-sitter didn't notice one day when my baby fell out of his stroller. Cara came in from picking up my daughter at school and found the baby screaming on the floor where he had landed. The new baby-sitter was asleep in the next room. After that I let Cara do all the jobs in my household and at the end of the week I went to the bank and paid her in stacks of crisp hundreds—the big bills were worth more in her home country. About this time, my father's journals were bought for posthumous publication, and our family split the money paid for them by Knopf. One of my brothers bought a house. My mother is still living on the money she invested. I paid Cara. It was worth every penny. Cara did so well that her children built a huge house with lots of marble and French doors. They sent us a video of the place. They called it "the house that James built" because it was baby-sitting for my son, James, that paid for everything.

Late one night the phone rang. "I can't tell you who I am," said a whispered voice, "but I wanted you to know that when your baby-sitter goes to pick up your daughter, she leaves your son unattended in his stroller in the street."

"Who is this?"

"A concerned mother." And that was all she would say. Naturally a million alarms went off in my head. I spent the rest of the night call-ing, and being reassured by, other mothers who were around the same school at pickup time. I didn't sleep. I carefully asked Cara, trying not to accuse her, if there was any chance that she had let James in his stroller out of her sight. She denied it absolutely. For a few weeks I hung around the school at pickup time, pretending that I happened to be walking by. Cara never let James alone for a moment as far as I could see. I still don't know what the truth was.

Later I found out who had called me that night and she didn't seem particularly crazy. It's the whole situation that's crazy. That a woman who has left her own children behind should be asked to ma-neuver two young children in a strange culture—knowing that any complaints she has will be met with irritation—is as insane as a situa-tion can be.

I had learned something from Juana. I knew that my feelings about Cara were about the situation rather than her behavior. I knew that I needed to pay her well for doing the most important job in my life. Still, the day she told me that she had taken a job in the New York City public school system was probably one of the worst days of my life. I felt helpless and betrayed. Even when I learned that Cara had jeopardized her new job by staying with me longer than she should have, I was unappeased. What about me? What about my kids? The pressures of handing my children over to another woman were still keeping me from being a decent human being. I was also sunk in self-pity. I had to work and maintain a career and take care of children at the same time. My mother hadn't had to do that. It was unfair, and my friends and peers who were in the same situation agreed. We are a generation of women who can feel very sorry for ourselves because we have to do what the generation before us didn't have to do. That self-pity blinded me to the feelings and situations of other people around me.

The last real baby-sitter I employed was Dominique. I believe that with Dominique, I was meant to learn what was really going on between me and my children's baby-sitters. She had left her own daughter behind in her home country when she came to New York, and after she worked for me for two years she got a full-time job with a couple downstairs who had just had a baby. Once again I was suffused with self-pity and anger. Nevertheless, I reluctantly gave her my blessing. About a year after that, a magazine asked me to write a profile of a nanny, and after some searching I settled on Dominique.

It was through this—through my work—that I was able to hear Dominique's story—a story that was probably a lot like Juana's story and Cara's story. I went to her apartment in Brooklyn. I hung out with Dominique and her friends. I got to be friends with Dominique myself, and she told me what it was like to work as a baby-sitter. She and her friends told me their horror stories about women who might have been my friends. I heard all about the irrational anger—from the point of view of the object of that anger. I heard all about the cheapness. I heard about the Lady Bountiful syndrome. I heard how it felt when an employer dismissed the findings of your doctor and insisted that you go to theirs—to a "real" doctor. I saw the way my grief and fear had made me oblivious to other women's problems.

We choose nannies who are completely one-dimensional to us. We don't know them or their families. We don't visit their homes or meet their children. Often we don't even speak their language. Then we underpay them. Then we trust them with our most precious possessions. We believe what we need to believe, which is that they love our children. We do this because, usually, we don't have a choice. Sometimes they do love our children.

Mothers and the baby-sitters who work for them are in painfully similar situations, but this similarity is obscured by surface appearances. The intense pain of letting a child be cared for by a stranger makes us mothers who have to do this literally crazy. It shuts down our humanity. We treat each other like cardboard cutouts; our families and the baby-sitters' families become like families of paper dolls. The unbearable pain of leaving a child behind to make money by caring for other people's children makes baby-sitters crazy. We will all stay crazy until the situation becomes a little more sane.

MY DAUGHTER SEARCHES FOR GOD

I TAUGHT MY DAUGHTER the Lord's Prayer, I arranged to have her christened, and I took her to church with me occasionally. With my son I have been less conscientious. He comes to church with me sometimes, just because I invite him. Even the forty-five-minute service gets boring for him, and he wanders out into the nave and plays with the verger or gets a head start on the coffee cake that we serve after communion sometimes. On Christmas Eve we all go to church to watch the Christmas Pageant, a thrilling performance involving some real baby sheep and a live donkey who once bucked off the Virgin Mary in a fit of holy exaltation. My son wears his best sweater and we sing carols. It makes me sad that he doesn't know the words to the songs—words which were engraved in my childhood brain long before I can even remember.

When my daughter was eleven, I was interviewing someone in Boston and I took her along for company. We stayed in Salem, Massachusetts, and visited the creaky witchcraft museum. We walked around Nathaniel Hawthorne's House of the Seven Gables. I told her the story of that book, and regaled her with edited stories of our ancestors who had come to the North Shore from Britain a long time before. I didn't tell her that one of our ancestors had been involved in the witchcraft trials, on the side of the judges. Instead I told her the stories about the

China trade that my grandmother had told me when I was a girl. I explained that they had set sail for China with coal and lumber and come home with holds filled with spices and silks and blue and white china used as ballast. I explained that that china, called Canton, was the china in her grandmother's house which had been handed down through generations of my father's family. Our visit to Boston was a lovely trip, and the last one we took for a long time. At the end of that year, my marriage began to come apart and we moved to an apartment a mile from the house where we had been living.

Soon after that my daughter turned to God in a big way—only the God she turned to was a different kind of God entirely. A friend had given her a book on witches. She began to read books about witches, about Salem, about Druids, and about other pagan religions. In the fifth grade, she formed a coven of four classmates and held meetings in her bedroom. Some of her friends were told by their parents that they couldn't join the coven. That didn't bother my daughter. Soon enough she had set up an altar with a variety of Wiccan artifacts. She found a store on the West Side devoted to various kinds of witchcraft, and she began to hang out there in her spare time. She saved up her allowance for a cauldron.

Her father and stepmother were worried. They banned witchcraft from their apartment. She decided—with much heartbreak all around—that she didn't want to spend the night there anymore. To console herself, she knelt for hours at the little altar in her room, burning candles and muttering odd prayers. By seventh grade, when she changed schools, her witchcraft was very entrenched. I told her she didn't have to mention it to the teachers at the Convent of the Sacred Heart. She made jokes about what Catholics did to witches, but she was undeterred. She took her altar on the school trip to visit Plymouth Rock.

Was I worried? Maybe I had so much else to worry about in those years that I wasn't paying attention, or maybe I had become a more tolerant woman. After all, as I explained to my daughter, this country that we live in is all about religious freedom. The Pilgrims landed on Plymouth Rock in their search for that freedom. Our First Amendment guarantees our right to say what we want and believe in what we want. I tried to help her worship when I could. I offered her a closet for her altar. I also decided that her witchcraft was part of a spiritual search. From what I heard, it sounded as if the woman who ran the witchcraft store was intelligent and sane. Coincidentally, I discovered that I knew and liked the woman's mother.

I thought my daughter was looking for something to believe in, and I admired her energy. I trusted her. The sisters at the convent agreed with me, in an example of true Christian charity. I am not Catholic, but the compassion, tolerance, and extraordinary teaching that goes on at the Convent of the Sacred Heart has made me a convert at least to Catholic education.

Nuns are a kind of running joke in our society. We have singing nuns and flying nuns, and art critic nuns, but they are, in fact, strong women who have pledged their lives to something larger than the material goals our society values so much. They are swimming upstream. The vows of poverty, chastity, and obedience—vows which were thought to be holy for centuries—are now out of fashion. We live in a world where everyone wants to make money, everyone wants to get laid, and everyone wants to do it their way. Follow your dreams, we say. So much for the ancient vows of holiness, so much for the sacred idea that service to God—or anything—should take precedence over our own individual happiness.

I told my daughter that she wasn't allowed to invite stray spirits into my apartment with her Ouija board—that would be like bringing homeless people in off the street for a snack, I said. I took her seriously. I respected her convictions. One thing I know for sure is that I don't know much, especially when it comes to religion. My own spiritual path is nothing to brag about. Slowly, Liley began to lose interest in witchcraft. She became too busy to go to the West Side. In the end, she never got a cauldron. Instead, she began talking with a young woman at school who happened to be a Mormon.

Pretty soon my daughter was reading The Book of Mormon, expatiating on Joseph Smith and attending the three-hour Mormon service at the Mormon temple near Lincoln Center every Sunday. She was almost fourteen, a time when many kids her age are seduced by the lure of drugs, alcohol, and sexual activity. Mormons don't drink alcohol or caffeine. They don't smoke, and they worship the family. That was all right with me. Liley gave up Diet Coke to be a Mormon. She began to have a new group of friends who called her every day. They offered to help her get to church if she needed transportation. They suggested she go on a retreat with them. I still don't know much about Mormonism, but I began to suspect that I, a twice divorced and once separated single mother was not exactly the Mormon female ideal.

My daughter went to the Church of Jesus Christ of the Latter-day Saints every Sunday. She had a routine. She would walk across the park, go to the service, and then buy herself a scone before heading home. I began to understand that my daughter was on some kind of journey. I suggested that she "interview" the minister at my own Episcopal church for a school project. She liked him. She went to communion a few times. She began to chafe against the authoritarian nature of the Mormon church. She didn't like their condemnation of divorce, and she was offended by their condemnation of homosexuality. She decided that she was going to embrace Judaism. She began going to Friday night services at a local synagogue.

I could easily have stopped all this. I could have agreed with her father. I could have forbidden my daughter from going to the West Side, either for witchcraft or for Mormonism. Because I knew I could, I didn't have to. Authority, real authority, is infinitely flexible. It doesn't pick fights. My daughter was inconveniencing me, but she wasn't torturing me. She wasn't hurting anyone. She was serious about trying to find a faith she could live with, and I was able to respect her seriousness—even when we also laughed about it. I began to refer to whatever she believed in as her religion of the month.

One of the things that has saved our family from disasters over and over again is our sense of humor. My daughter's religions didn't threaten me because I saw them as the questioning of a young girl looking for a real faith. Sure I wished she had found a faith—my faith—but in the meantime I was content that she cared enough to look.

"Aren't you worried about her?" my friends would say, when I described her expeditions to stores which specialized in enchantments, or her poring over Mormon tracts. Sometimes I was, but I was certainly less worried than if she had been searching for the perfect clothes or the perfect boyfriend, or even the perfect grades.

Slowly she began to drift toward Christianity. We started taking turns going to my church, and she made friends with the minister. She was also involved with the community service structure in her school—a structure closely allied with the Catholic sisters. She began to study the Bible and Christianity. She was fascinated by religion courses. She read about the Buddha and Allah. She wrote a paper on Dorothy Day. She read Teilhard de Chardin and St. Augustine. She did a paper on New York City's variety of religious communities. She began studying the Bible in a new way; as she grew into becoming a feminist, she began to see the feminism in the Christian gospels.

This year she is wavering between being Episcopalian and being Catholic. In the meantime she has become a well-informed theologian herself. As it turned out, her spiritual search led not to any religion, but to a passionate interest in spiritual search. My daughter has a calling. She'll go to the college with the best Bible study and theology department she can find. She wants to get a divinity degree and study the Bible in Greek and Hebrew. She's the most focused student in her class. She has opened dialogues, on e-mail and through regular mail, with adults who have written and thought about personal faith. She goes up to the West Side to interview teachers at the Union Theological Seminary. Now she's saving her allowance for college.

What's scary is how easy it would have been to abuse my parental authority and stop her search. Who knew that a fifth-grade coven would end up as an estimable career? I sure didn't. Who knew that every religion she tried added to her knowledge and experience in what turns out to be her chosen field of work and study? In order to be good parents, we have to keep a distance from our children's roller-coaster emotions. We have to have a sense of humor about things that may seem deadly serious to them. They are children, caught up in the early part of this journey of self-discovery. We are older, farther along, and we can share our experience, but that's often all we can do.

One of the results of my own spiritual search has been the realization that, if there is a God—and I believe there is—that God is not me. I believe that each person, including my daughter, has his or her own God, and that many matters are best left to that higher authority. There are many, many things that we can't know—among them what's going to happen tomorrow, what is going to happen tonight, and even what is going to happen right now. Part of being an adult is having the humility to admit the limits of adult authority. It's my belief that many parents have abdicated their parental authority, while others exceed it. It's as if we don't want the responsibility of the power we have because we prefer to long for the power we don't have—the power we can only pretend to have.

PART TWO

RABBIT IN THE SNOW

LATE ON A WINTER NIGHT, with my son asleep in the passenger seat and my daughter dozing in the back, I was maneuvering our rented car down an icy hill in northern Vermont. My son had spent the evening with a friend. My daughter had come to a reading of mine in Manchester. As the road curved steeply down Green Peak toward the valley, my headlights picked up a dark form at the edge of the piles of snow which bordered the road. "Mom, look!" my daughter shouted, suddenly sitting forward. I gingerly braked the car and came to a slippery stop. The amorphous form became a large rabbit—a hare really—blinking in the brightness. It seemed to be looking right at us. I immediately thought about driving on. It was too late at night to stop. The hill was steep. The rabbit was clearly hurt. Let nature take care of its own, I thought. "Hey, it's a rabbit and he's hurt," said my suddenly wide-awake son. "We have to help him."

"This is a bad place to stop." I thought about all the reasons that wild creatures are better off left alone. I remembered what had happened to Jack Nicholson in the movie *Wolf*. I looked out through the car windows at the dangers of the freezing night and the January snow. What if another car came down the hill behind us and couldn't stop? What if our car started to slide? What if the animal who had injured the rabbit was waiting just off stage in the darkness? I set the emergency brake. Slipping on the ice I got out of the car and walked to where the animal was bleeding slightly in the snow. It didn't seem badly hurt. I could see that it was a hare, with powerful back legs and small front legs. One of the front legs jutted out at an odd angle. Because of this, when the rabbit hopped, it turned in a useless circle. Left alone, it would certainly freeze to death. I got back in the car and reached for the emergency brake. Then I hesitated for a second too long.

"Let's just keep going," I said, but my daughter had already peeled off her sweater. I wasn't quite fast enough, or quite certain enough, to stop her when she stepped out into the snow, scooped up the wounded rabbit, and climbed back into the car. The warmth of the car and my daughter's gentle touch seemed to soothe the rabbit and it stopped trying to hop. "The poor little bunny," my son cooed. "Don't worry. We'll take care of you. You're safe now."

"We couldn't just leave it there," my daughter said, seeing that I still had doubts and perhaps having a rational moment herself. "It looks as if it was dropped by a hawk or owl or something. I think this front leg is broken. Shhhh, lie still."

I released the brake and began the treacherous trip down the rest of the hill to Route 7 at the bottom. "Let's take him to the vet!" my son suggested. It was late at night, long after most country veterinarians had closed. For a brief, mad moment I thought about going to the local hospital emergency room. Then I realized what kind of reception we would get.

"We'll take it home and make it comfortable if we can," I said, refusing to call the rabbit "he." "Then in the morning we'll see what we should do." The kids and the rabbit were quiet as we drove south toward Bennington. Above us I could see Orion in the winter sky and a half-moon on the far horizon. I thought of other rabbits in my life. I remembered Peter Rabbit in Beatrix Potter's tale, and the way Peter's father met with an accident in Mr. McGregor's garden. I wondered what sort of accident our rabbit met with in the snowy night. I thought about my childhood pet rabbit Sylvia (named after the writer Sylvia Townsend Warner), who met with an accident when an inebriated friend of my father's sat on the chair cushion under which she liked to hide. I remembered spending Christmas in Nantucket when we all got drunk, went out and jacked rabbits, shooting them as they froze in the headlights of the jeep, and made rabbit stew for dinner. I remembered my daughter's rabbit, Smoky—named for the fire my husband had set in our Manhattan house while enjoying a gift bottle as he cooked the Christmas goose.

When we came on the rabbit on the hillside that night, we were on the way home from a reading of my memoir, *Note Found in a Bottle.* In the book I describe the way alcoholism distorted our life as a family. Now, as I drove, I wondered if I was crazy to pick up an injured wild rabbit in the middle of the night. Perhaps I was trying to make some sort of amends to my children and to all of us for all those other drunken accidents with all those other rabbits.

Back indoors at Bennington, we made a bed for the rabbit in a dresser drawer and gave it a dish of cool water and a few potato chips— the only thing in our kitchen. During the night, while we slept, it quietly died. In the morning I comforted the children, wrapped the rabbit's body in a towel, and put it on the floor in our kitchen. Later in the day, after class, I borrowed a shovel.

As the afternoon waned, when the children were busy sledding, I took the rabbit in one hand and the shovel in the other and walked deep into the woods on the crusty snow. Near a group of maples I found some rabbit paw prints. There I dug a shallow grave in the snow and the frozen ground. The digging and the late afternoon sun made everything seem golden and warm. As I lowered the rabbit into its grave I said a prayer for its spirit and for the spirit of all living things.

I'm still not sure I did the right thing. I've come to realize that when it comes to situations with my children, there often is no right thing. Would I have stopped for a mole or an opossum? Probably not. Would I have stopped for a skunk? Definitely not. What would I have done if the animal by the side of the road was a dog wearing a collar? Why would I have picked it up then without questions? Is one life more valuable than another? Is the life of a domesticated animal worth more than the life of a wild animal? Am I so sentimental that a rabbit— with its connotations of Easter bunnies and cute little pets—seems more important than a less attractive animal?

These are important questions, but they are questions I can't begin to answer. I only know that at that moment—the moment when I might have released the emergency brake and started on down the hill—I stopped. Perhaps I was afraid of my children's feelings. Perhaps I imagined my son later weeping for the rabbit whom he would imagine dying out there in the snow. Furthermore, the rabbit might have been better off without our help. On the other hand there are those who believe that animals are reincarnations of ourselves—so perhaps we did help in giving it a more comfortable death. For reasons I can't really explain, once we had seen the rabbit, leaving it there to die would have been an act of brutality.

It didn't matter that we were projecting our own feelings onto the rabbit and that there is even a name for this—the pathetic fallacy. An act of brutality is an act of brutality. A life is a life. It's true that in other situations we eat animals which are brutally killed, or that I might buy a rabbit's foot for one of my children as a good luck charm. Each situation has its own morality, that's what makes doing the right thing so complicated. As children get older—as they do in the second half of this book—the things they learn are hard to teach. Telling children the difference between right and wrong sounds easy, and sometimes it is. It's right to share and wrong to bite. Do unto others as you would have them do unto you. Love thy neighbor as thyself. But right and wrong sometimes shift around with different circumstances. I want my children to know right from wrong—sure. Even more importantly, though, I want them to be able to tease out the more right from the more wrong in complicated situations. I hope to teach them that right and wrong are sometimes as clear as a sunny afternoon, and sometimes as slippery as an icy road on a winter night.

Comforts

When my son is feeling shaky, he jumps onto my big bed, centers himself, and curls his body into a tight ball. It's a ritual we have been practicing for almost seven years now, and I know just what to do.

"Oh, an egg!" I say. "There's an egg on my bed! What an amazing egg!" I pretend to be surprised and delighted. I throw up my hands in astonishment and dance around the bed. If there is anyone else at home, I urge them loudly to come into my room and look at this incredible egg. "Look at this beautiful egg!" I exclaim. At this point I begin to stroke my son's back and his head. "What a soft, unusual shell," I say. "What a lovely egg." The egg is motionless. "I wonder what kind of egg this could be," I say breathlessly. "It's too big for a chicken egg." In the years we have been playing this game, my son has gone from being a toddler to being a tall ten-year-old. "It's too small for a dinosaur egg," I say. "I wonder how it got here?"

At this point, after everyone around has duly appreciated the presence of this magnificent egg, the egg begins to shiver slightly and rock back and forth. "Oh my goodness, it's hatching!" I shout. "It's hatching." The egg hatches with exquisite slowness, using many of the techniques studied by my son's class in watching a brood of chicks hatch in an incubator early in his academic career. The animal within pecks against the shell with its egg tooth—my son's nose. First its arms push out through the invisible shell and then its legs. At first its eyes are shut. "It's hatching, it's hatching," I say excitedly. "I think it's a baby dinosaur, no it's a frog, no it's a puppy!" With an almost imperceptible nod my son acknowledges what he has decided to be when hatched. Finally the baby animal's eyes open. I give it a big hug. "Welcome to our world," I say. The baby animal bounds off my bed and prances around the room.

When she feels shaky, my daughter curls up with Real Me. She makes the noise I tell her she made when she was an infant. "Meep, meep," she says, and she asks me to read a Margaret Wise Brown book I read her way back then. I've always thought that this book, *The Runaway Bunny,* with its mystical imaginings, was about maternal tenacity. In it the little bunny keeps running away and its mother keeps finding it anyway. My daughter tells me that she thinks the book is about God.

Comfort rituals are one of childhood's great pleasures. When I was a child, I loved to rub my nose with a blue blanket, pick a fuzz ball off it, and curl up with my thumb in my mouth. This drove my parents nuts. They took away the blanket. They promised me a puppy if I stopped sucking my thumb. I stopped. They bought a puppy. I was allergic to the puppy. She went back to the kennel and my thumb went back in my mouth. My thumb was coated with iodine. I sucked it off. I was threatened with buck teeth. I didn't care. My thumb was tied into a gauze mitten. I sucked right through it. No one was going to separate me from my thumb.

I wonder where the line is between the comfort rituals of childhood with their quirky charm, and the comfort rituals of adulthood which can often be so self-destructive. Maybe there's no difference. Maybe in encouraging my children to comfort themselves I am laying the foundation for a life of crime. Maybe my parents were right to think that thumb sucking was right up there with lying to parents and cruelty to peers. Having ways to calm and comfort ourselves is part of learning to live as adults. I'm just trying to take the edge off; that's what people say when they have that second martini, or that chocolate bar, or when they sleep with the wrong person. I was just looking for a bit of oblivion.

Of course there's a big distance between my son acting out his innocent hatching drama, and the kind of comfort that ends up in destruction, death, and emotional chaos. One of the things I hope my children learn is to tell the difference between innocent comfort and comfort which puts its fist through the thin skin of a harmonious universe. In order to teach our children right from wrong, we have to figure out for ourselves what's right and wrong. In order to help our children grow into adult comfort rituals, we have to know and understand the true adult sources of comfort.

There are many real sources of comfort and delight in the world: there is the glory of nature, the beauty of a lake shimmering on a summer day or a winter sunset, there are the sensual joys of beautiful things, of wonderful food, of exercise and the intense joy of getting lost in a great book or piece of music. Everything from the New Testament to Edith Wharton, from James Taylor to Beethoven have been great sources of comfort for me. But really—and it took me years to figure this out, although it has been the basis of almost every moral code since men and women emerged from the primeval ooze—the true sources of comfort for me are love and service. I am comforted by a connection to another human being whether it is a lover or a stranger or one of my children. I am comforted when I am able to be useful to another human being, whoever it is. I also find it deeply comforting to remember to live one day at a time, and this is also the tenet of thousands of belief systems. One day, today, is all anyone is sure of, and I like to remember that. Most of all I get, as an adult, tremendous comfort from God, and from my friends who believe in God.

Bears and eggs and thumbs are all very well for a while, but as children grow into adults they need to find other ways to feel contented in this uncomfortable world of ours. Part of being a grown-up is to understand how distinctly uncomfortable life can be. Our children need to know that we understand, and that we know how much they need comfort because we need comfort too. I hope my kids will learn to share my comforts, comforts which are incredibly lasting, which are dependent on God, and which never have the fur worn off or lose their button eyes.

MY SON'S FEARS are as irrational as his comforts. What children like is often strange, but what they dislike can be even stranger. For a long time, on our trips to the market my son steered me away from the dairy department, where cases of milk and yogurt are the background for huge wheels of cheese, some whole and stacked on top of each other, and some cut into sections and shrink-wrapped for sale. "Let's get out of here, Mom," my son would say when I headed that way. My son was afraid of the wheels of cheese. He didn't like the largeness of the wheels. He doesn't like anything that has pieces cut from it—remember the chocolate cake in Grand Central Terminal?

My daughter was not just afraid of costumes and masks. She was also terrified of garden shears. I had to wait until she was asleep to take them out of the drawer and trim the dead leaves on our houseplants. When I was growing up, my brother was afraid of buttons. If I came to the family breakfast table wearing buttons—inadvertently, of course— he would hold a napkin up in front of his face and eat by slipping food under its lower edge in order to avoid looking at me and my buttons. "It's not buttons," my father would inevitably explain to no one in particular. "What he's really afraid of are nipples! Women's nipples!" This didn't seem to comfort my brother very much.

Perhaps because of this embarrassment I tried to keep my fears secret. As a child I could hardly bear to be in the same room with an ashtray or any cigarette butts. The smell of tobacco made me nauseated. This may seem like good sense now, but at the time everyone smoked. My father smoked Camels. My mother smoked Chesterfields. When no one was looking I would slyly empty their ashtrays, trying not to watch the horrible cigarette butts as they slipped into the garbage. There was something creepy about cigarette butts and ashes that made it impossible for me to coexist with them. Slowly, because I had to, I overcame the flesh-crawling, stomach-churning feeling I associated with cigarettes and smoking.

Sometimes I forget how alien children are from everything we grown-ups take for granted. They are like creatures from another planet. One of my son's classmates always has to wear a certain hat, another is afraid of moths, a third won't go to the movies because he doesn't want to sit in that big dark theater. For years my daughter wouldn't go out without a small plastic dog named Gloria—named after the dog in a book she loved called *No Flying in the House*.

When I casually, in a relaxed moment, ask my son why he might be afraid of wheels of cheese, he tries to explain. They are too big. If there were a lot of them, they might run him over. They could roll. His fear, like all childhood fears including my own, seems irrational to me. I know my job is to teach my children to be at home in the world—a world where wheels of cheese are signs of abundance and costumes are signs of fun. Sometimes I wonder if I am wrong. Perhaps wheels of cheese *are* dangerous. Maybe he knows something that I have blocked out. Maybe he was an unhappy dairy farmer in a past life. At any rate, these fears are real. I try to comfort my children. I also try to teach them to comfort themselves.

DOES MONEY HELP?

WHEN MY FATHER CAME BACK from World War II, he brought a handsome uniform, a few souvenirs from the Pacific, and a way of life that was based on rules and regulations. My earliest relationship with him revolved around his re-creations of army life, with him as the sergeant, and me as the naughty four-year-old private. "Tennshun!" he would bark, and whatever I was doing, I would snap to attention, my spine straight, my little hand raised in a perfect salute. "March!" he would command, and I would start down the living room toward the windows looking out at the Queensboro Bridge. "Quarter turn!" I would change direction and head for the bedroom. "Half turn!" Now I was marching toward the kitchen. "KP duty!" he would snap, and I would delightedly wash the dishes—a task I otherwise abhorred. "At ease, Private Cheever," my father would say with a sigh, signaling the end of our game. In a moment I'd be begging to play again.

When we were at ease though, my father rarely gave orders. I grew up in a family where money was sometimes scarce, and authority was always scarce. Not only did my mother read Dr. Spock's myth-shattering *Baby and Child Care,* but she had known Ben Spock while she was growing up on the Yale college campus—her father was dean of the medical school—and thought he was an intelligent fellow. My parents were as charming and friendly as children our own age, but they also seemed confused and lost when life got complicated. When we couldn't afford something I wanted, it often seemed to hurt my parents as much as it hurt me. Except for financial restrictions, there were never any limits on where I could go or what I could do. My parents seemed to believe that I knew how to behave as well as they did.

They had authoritarian parents, the kind of adults who told them what to do, and who punished them when they didn't do it. I learned most things the hard way, blundering into situations which were sometimes dangerous and sometimes just horrendously embarrassing. My parents didn't even pretend to give me orders for living. I envied my parents' friends who were strict and laid down the law. Often my parents didn't seem to know the law, or else they thought the law was stupid, not for us, hardly worth bothering to defy. There were exceptions to this laxness: table manners, household chores, and most of all bedtime.

BY THE TIME I was in elementary school, the most glamorous girl in my class was not the rich one who lived in the old Keyes mansion, or the pretty one whose handsome daddy picked her up after school in his convertible, or the graceful one who danced Clara in the school performance of The Nutcracker—it was the girl who had no bedtime. While the rest of us were forced into an odious routine of baths, pleading for glasses of water, and the final terrifying darkness when the lights were turned out, our classmate stayed up chatting with her parents, fixing herself snacks, and heading up to bed when she felt like it.

In the summer, bedtime was a travesty. It was still daylight when the axe fell. I would lie in bed listening to the grown-ups sitting outdoors in the fragrant evening with their friends and their martinis, and fume at the injustice of my situation. After a few drinks, they were fond of answering my protests by reciting a Robert Louis Stevenson poem I came to hate. "In winter I get up at night and dress by yellow candlelight. In summer quite the other way, I have to go to bed by day," they would chant, as if Victorian children had anything to do with me growing up in the Hudson River suburbs of New York City.

In winter, bedtime was scary. I spent the evening dreading the moment when I would be left alone in the dark. Outside my window the pines moved in the wind in the implacable night. I could sense danger building under my bed, and in the blackness in the corners of the room, and in the closet behind the half-closed closet door. My walls came alive with mysterious sounds and shadows. The roof creaked. I lay awake staring at the ceiling and listening to my frightened heartbeat. I tried to think of children in other countries on the other side of the world who were still playing happily in the afternoon sun. The earliest bedtime prayer I learned confirmed my fear. "If I die before I wake," it said, as if this was a real possibility recognized by all thinking people.

As a parent, decades later, I discovered something about bedtime that was never explained to me as a child. It might have helped. Bedtime is not the way parents impose their own superior will on their oppressed children. That wasn't my parents' style anyway. They were all sail and no anchor, as the great historian Thomas Macaulay wrote of the United States Constitution in 1857. Bedtime is the anchor of every parent's day. It is the way parents keep their own sanity. It's not a rule which is imposed to infringe the rights of children; it's a rule which preserves the rights of parents.

The essence of good parenting is not quality time, it's quantity time. "Child raising is not some mysterious process; adults have been engaged in it since the beginning of time, long before we had experts or manuals," write Sylvia Ann Hewlett and Cornel West in their powerful book, *The War Against Parents*. "At the heart of the matter is time, huge amounts of it, freely given." West and Hewlett make the point that parents struggle to raise their children in our country in a society which is fiercely discriminatory against parents. Everything, from the tax code to the media, makes our job harder. "The Zeitgeist of American culture has become profoundly antagonistic against parents," they write. It's still our job. I spend, as my parents did, so much time with my children and their friends, in classrooms, helping with math homework and term papers, playing with blocks or makeup, shopping for pajamas with dinosaurs on them or for dance dresses, that I like to joke that I need to care for my "inner adult." Bedtime is when I do that.

A lot of my best parenting decisions have been made when I thought about the quality of the lives involved, especially my own. A lot of my worst and most frustrating decisions have been made when I tried to get my kids to follow someone else's schedule. This is what I

call the "should" school of parenting. I have found that I can drive myself crazy trying to get my kids to do things on my schedule or Dr.
Spock's schedule or anyone else's schedule—only to find they have
their own schedules and I might as well save my breath. Still, in balancing my life as a mother with the rest of my life, I have made many
painful mistakes. One of the worst was when my daughter was about
four years old, and her father and I often entertained.

At our dinner parties my daughter, dressed in her adorable nightgown, was allowed to pass the canapés. One dreadful night I found her,
just as the guests were about to arrive, playing with a half-empty bottle
of my thyroid pills. There was no way of knowing how many she had
taken. When I asked her, she gave me a vague, four-year-old's answer. I
called the pediatrician, who ordered me to dose her with Ipecac. Better
safe than sorry, he said. I had no idea of the effects of Ipecac on a four-
year-old child. It was too late to cancel the party; the guests were on
their way. My daughter began to throw up just as they sat down to dinner. I spent the evening shuttling between the dining room, where
chicken breasts with morels were being followed by chocolate deca-
dence, and the bedroom, where my little girl was heaving with sobs and
throwing up everything in her stomach every twenty minutes. It was
one of the most horrible nights of my life.

We lived an expensive life in those days. My daughter's elaborate
birthdays were videotaped. When my daughter's best friend got her
own pony, we all felt that my daughter was suffering from deprivation.
When I bought my daughter an absurdly expensive dress and matching
shoes for an Easter party, a friend of mine pooh-poohed my attack of
conscience.

"Three hundred dollars for a kid's outfit?" I said.

"She has to have something to wear," said my friend.

My son has grown up in very different circumstances. I sold the
apartment soon after he was born, and since then I have had to stop
thinking of money as a limitless commodity. My son has never had a
private lesson of any kind. He goes to public school. His clothes are
strictly functional, and most of them have holes in them. Instead of having a rotating crew of help and baby-sitters, I have occasional baby-
sitters and a cleaning lady who comes in every other week. This is what
I would call a truly privileged life.

When she was young I wasn't sure I knew how to take care of my daughter. My passion for her was mixed with fear. Because we had a great deal of help, I wasn't forced to learn that I did know how to take care of her. The truth is that money insulates things—that's what's good about it and that's what's bad about it. All the things we had when my daughter was little, all the help and all the trips and all the dinner parties and all the expectations, insulated me from some of the terrors and some of the joys of raising a child. My daughter often kissed me good night when I was in evening clothes and on my way out. Once or twice I even warned her not to mess up my hair. My son usually says good night to me when we are all in our pajamas. We share a snack before turning in. I stay awake and read and work, but I'm right there and he knows it. I take him to school every morning and I pick him up every afternoon.

In many ways I think that having limited money, as I have in the past decade, has been a huge help in raising both my children. For one thing I am careful to live within our income. My children see that I get receipts and balance the books every month. They also see me at work, so they can understand the correspondence between how much I work and how much I earn. When one of my children wants something expensive, I don't say yes or no. We sit down and talk about the expense. We plot and plan ways to get the thing—whether it's a laptop computer that my daughter needs or a new bicycle for my son—at the lowest possible price. We try to figure out how to pay for it: Will Granny help? How much is in their savings accounts? Can I spring for an advance on allowances? Because we don't have a lot of money, my children are intimately involved with the family financial decisions.

I see that in other families, wealthier families, money can cause plenty of trouble. If there are unlimited funds, parents' decisions about what children can or cannot have seem arbitrary. Unlimited money, or seemingly unlimited money, puts parents in a difficult position. Too much power is as difficult to handle as too little power. In our family this doesn't happen. The fact that we don't have a lot of money has helped me teach my children about a kind of reality that I only too recently learned myself.

Our modest, visible budget also gives me tremendous leverage because my children know how quickly their privileges could be suspended. Every month I pay the phone bill. It's always high. I know that by taking away my daughter's phone I can reduce that expense, and she knows that too. So when I do have to exert my authority, I have easy ways to do it. In relation to money, our lives make sense, it seems to me, and what could be more valuable than that?

CLOTHES

BEFORE I HAD A BABY, I HAD BABY CLOTHES. Although I had no idea what was about to happen to me when I gave birth, I might have known by the number of outfits I bought for myself in the last few months of my pregnancy—three—and the number of outfits I bought for the baby who kicked against my stomach and gave me the giggles by having hiccups at the most inopportune moments—about two thousand. My transformation from child to adult was already happening, in my closet. In pregnancy I chose clothes for their durability. When they had lived out their usefulness—a green winter coat that I wore every day, for instance—I never wanted to see them again. The hope and sentimentality I was used to investing in clothes fell away as my body got bigger than I had ever imagined a body could get. Instead I shopped for my baby.

I began with a basic layette, a bassinet filled with stretchies and receiving blankets. I knew that wasn't enough, though. I had read somewhere about the mother who bought a full layette—thinking that it would last for months—and found that at the end of the baby's first day at home all the clothes had been used. Babies change clothes as often as fashion models during design week. At the baby shower I picked up another suitcase filled with clothes, including a beautiful lavender lace dress and embroidered smocked dresses of Irish lace and linen that were far finer than anything I would ever have bought for myself. Baby dresses are beautiful things; babies very sweetly destroy whatever they wear. As Easter approached, my daughter's room filled with piles of stuffed animals and her closet and dresser bulged with spun cotton and soft, light wool. She had a crib, a bassinet, a carrying basket, and a bouncinette, all waiting for her as if it might never be necessary to hold her. "I've never known a baby to have so many beds," my father said when he saw her room. I didn't dare show him her clothes.

When she was a toddler, I still spent more time buying her clothes than I did buying my own clothes. Who can blame me? Children's clothes are some of the most adorable and delicious objects in the world. I bought her tiny cotton jumpers in flower patterns trimmed with grosgrain ribbon, and corduroy dresses with plaid sashes and trim. I indulged in pale pink tights and ballerina skirts. Handknit sweaters with ribbon woven through the wool, thick velvet pinafores, forget-me-knots printed on matching T-shirts and cotton lawn skirts, a blue wool coat with a peaked hood and frog fastenings, all made their way into my daughter's closet, and sometimes onto her increasingly reluctant body.

By the time she could express herself, though, her clothing preferences had become vivid and particular. Her helplessness ended, fast. When she turned two, she decided that she could only wear pink. This required a new wardrobe of pale pinks and deep pink sweaters. A few months later, though, she decided that she could never wear pink again. Pink was the color she hated the most. Why had I bought her all this pink? The pink was pushed to the back of her closet to make room for navy and deep red and—her new favorite—plaid. Within a year, though, plaid became anathema. She disliked plaid and she detested any of the colors usually found in plaid—red, green, blue, and yellow.

The year she turned five was the year she fell in love with black. Everything had to be black. Sometimes I was able to sneak a little gray or navy blue into her wardrobe, but black was her favorite. When her bedroom was repainted, she furiously, definitely wanted it to be painted black and she wanted a black carpet to match. I told her that the store had run out of black paint. Maybe that was a mistake. She's eighteen now and she's still wearing black.

Once she was able to dress herself, I tried to institute a different kind of rule. No holes and no spots. I tried to let everything else go. I tried to remember that Liley is not me, that she is a separate person with a right to her own desires and preferences and even the right to express those desires and preferences in her clothes—more or less. Sometimes, when she would get ready to go to her grandmother's in faded shorts, or head off to a school assembly in sweats, I interceded. Mostly, I let go. I tried to pick my battles, and I decided that I would not let clothes become a battleground. Raising children is an exercise in prioritizing and reprioritizing—with money and everything else. What is really important is the children's health, safety, and peace of mind. Everything else is much less important. Things that once seemed critical like cleanliness, neatness, even stylishness, slowly and inexorably shift to the bottom of the list.

Clothes have the power to transform. Clothes also serve as powerful symbols of who we are and who we want to be. They are our fastest and most malleable means of self-expression. The first thing anyone sees is how we look—we can't have much control over the basics, but we can choose what we will wear. And we can also—for a while—choose what our children will wear. Even as I searched for transformation for myself, I searched for self-expression in dressing my daughter. My daughter was my sartorial tabula rasa. Each year she had a new broad-brimmed Easter hat with a wide ribbon and matching patent leather Mary Janes. Struggling to take her emerging preferences into account and still accommodate my own fantasies I swathed her in fashion.

After Liley's father and I divorced there was much less money for clothes, and within a few years there was so little money that I strained to buy her the new shoes she needed every three months. I like to think that I would have learned not to dress my children as part of my image—my image of how our family should look—if we hadn't bottomed out financially. I doubt it. It seems so innocent. I want my family to look like the family in my dreams. It's only when it's clear that the family is made up of different people with different tastes and ideas that it becomes less innocent. A family is like any other group of people in that the good of each member has to be balanced with the good of the whole.

During the years when making the money to pay the rent and buy healthy food took up all of my energies, it became dramatically less important to me what any of us wore. My daughter, who had a drawerful of pajamas with pink hearts on them and nightgowns with frilly lace and cute prints, often slept in an oversized T-shirt. When our little family was prosperous again, I found that I had changed the way I felt about my children's clothes. My son's clothes have always been more functional than fashionable. Not for him the obligatory trip to the boy's department of a fancy store to be humiliated by salespeople. He has never been to Brooks Brothers, and he doesn't seem to mind!

My son doesn't like to shop for clothes. Clothes are not on his Christmas list. As far as my son is concerned, clothes are necessary but unimportant. All of his tastes in clothes are about establishing that he is a boy. He won't wear any color—yellow, purple—which might be construed as feminine. I dress my son in polo shirts and sweats and every year I buy him one fancy sweater for special occasions. He doesn't have a blue blazer for wearing with the Brooks shirt and tie that many of his peers have. He doesn't want them and I don't insist. I want him to be comfortable, clean, and neat—beyond that anything goes.

I let my daughter buy her own clothes now. If something is expensive, I ask her to find what she likes and put it on hold so that I can look at it before we take the plunge. My children both have wonderful friends, and one of my daughter's friends spends whole days shopping with her, helping her find what her tastes are when she decides not to wear black jeans and a black T-shirt. Usually the clothes she and my daughter find are breathtakingly beautiful, cut to show off the exuberance of their youthful bodies, the pale velvet of their skins, their long masses of shiny hair.

I have learned that if I want to look a certain way or if I want my family to look a certain way, I have to focus on myself. I can teach my children some basic rules. But I know that their clothes are their way of telling their own stories. My family is not a prop. My family is a group of beautiful and beloved individuals. When I see families who look the way I dreamed we might look some day—with their daughters in smocked dresses and pretty hats and their sons in blue blazers and little neckties— I have a pang of jealousy. Then I remember that I have the most wonderful children in the world. I wouldn't trade a second of my time with them, I wouldn't change a molecule of their beings. Parents who are grown-up don't hide behind their children. They don't use their children as fashion accessories. They restrict their fantasies to themselves.

THE PEDAGOGY OF PARENTING: HOW DO CHILDREN LEARN?

WHEN I WAS GROWING UP, a grown-up was the thing to be. The grown-ups in my world seemed infinitely glamorous and privileged. My parents in their everyday clothes—my father in a suit, tie shoes, and a felt hat, my mother in a dress with gloves and a hat, stockings and high heels—were formidable models of adulthood to which I deeply aspired. On car trips the grown-ups always sat in front. At mealtimes the grown-ups often sat at a separate table where they ate exotic grown-up foods. When I wanted to be with my parents, I knew that I had to do what they were doing. If I wanted to talk with them, I had to find a way to join their conversation. I learned to be polite at parties. I imitated them in every way I could. Thusly, I learned to read.

One of the things that makes raising children fascinating is watching how they learn. Just lately, for instance, I have bought a series of laminated table mats which display maps of the world, maps of the United States, charts of the solar system, and lists—with photographs and dates—of the forty-two American presidents. At dinner, after we say grace, we quiz each other on the contents of our mats. My son is usually the quizmaster and this makes the whole thing fun for him. He has power. He likes to take points off for gloating; I often end up losing on gloating points. My daughter and I struggle to answer his questions. When we come on something interesting—a president who served just one year in office, like James Garfield in 1881 for instance—I look it up in the dictionary of biography and read aloud. As a result of these mats, which we've had for about a year now, we have all learned more American history and geography than I ever knew before. My nine-year-old son knows why Grover Cleveland was elected twice—and who served in between his terms—what happened after Lincoln was assassinated, and the difference between the popular John Adams and the intellectual, dour John Quincy Adams and when each of them served. (They were the second and the sixth presidents respectively.)

This is what my son's school calls "top down" learning, learning done out of an intense personal desire for some other result—in this case the desire to dominate the dinner table. At my son's school, the kids are taught to read by being given books that are so interesting—this takes some finding and choosing, but that's the point—that they desperately want to read.

In the household where I grew up, my parents practiced this principle without even meaning to. One of the great privileges of being a grown-up was reading real books. My hunger to be an adult pushed me to books that were just at the edge of my comprehension. Reading was the one activity that always won approval from my parents. I remember my father's delighted amusement when, at age twelve, I faked sickness in order to stay at home and read Wilkie Collins's *The Woman in White*. I finished it in one long, delicious day, and the conversations I had about it with my father were almost as good as the book. After that I read anything my father cared about, from Dumas to Flaubert. At first it was my entrée into the adult world, and then it caught me. Reading is still my favorite thing to do.

WHAT STARTED AS A MIRROR of my own childhood has become one of my favorite parts of mothering my own children. I have a friend who assigns a book each summer to every member of her extended family. She buys the book for each of them and their discussions oil the creaky joints of the family when they get together. Reading together is a wonderful way to establish understanding. It's like going into couples therapy with Jane Austen or Charlotte Brontë; a brilliant third party is there to help you.

My daughter began to read early. At the age of five, she had a lyrical writing voice. Her poems were filled with startling natural images. Then, at the age of seven she discovered the vast literature which the book industry pumps out for young girls. That was the end of her natural voice. She read at least a book a day and the results were clear in her writing. Everything she wrote began more or less the same way. "Hi! My name is Tiffany Wells. I have green eyes and blond hair and I have a terrible crush on a cute guy named Craig who sits next to me in math class." Her idea of literature was what I call teen lit: a Hello Kitty calendar and a pile of paperbacks with titles like *Meet the Wakefield Twins* or *Prom Night*.

There is a lot of piety about books in our culture. Many people believe that all reading is good reading. I don't. Books are powerful and they can corrupt as well as they can inform. The summer of my daughter's fourth-grade year I fought against the pulp she was devouring by giving her a personal reading list. For her allowance, I asked her to read *Animal Farm* by George Orwell. She read it and hated it. Then I tried *Jane Eyre* by Charlotte Brontë. My daughter loved the character of Blanche Ingram, the smarmy beauty who schemes to marry Rochester for his money—a character right out of *Prom Night*. She thought the rest of the book was "just okay." In September she went back to school and dutifully read the usual fifth grade fare. The next summer I tried again, this time with Robert Louis Stevenson's *Treasure Island*. Liley read it the way she eats her vegetables—methodically and without joy.

Then I gave her a short, delicious Edith Wharton novel titled *Summer*. From the first page, she was hooked. She was hooked! She didn't want to come to dinner. She asked her friends if she could call them back later. That summer she read every Edith Wharton novel we could find, and she never looked back. "I haven't read any trash since then," she says. (Although last weekend I did notice my copy of *Bridget Jones's Diary* in her backpack.)

Last year I started the same process with my son. They say that reading aloud to your children helps them become readers. My son doesn't really like to have me read aloud. He'd rather play Nintendo. My son goes to a school where everyone reads, but the idea that he could read at home just because he wanted to eluded him. I bought books for him which piled up unread in his bookshelves. I took him to the children's room at the library. I treated him to his choice of anything he wanted at the bookstore. Last summer, on a trip through Hanover, New Hampshire, we stopped at the Dartmouth bookstore. His eyes lit up as he perused the shelves. "Mom! look at this!" He grabbed at it, a book titled *Captain Underpants*. He read the entire series, chuckling about the revenge of the talking toilets and the invasion of the evil cafeteria ladies.

After that he wanted to go to the bookstore where we discovered Mary Pope Osborne's *Treehouse* series. My son read story after story while dust gathered on the television set. On the pretext that the library might have books in the *Treehouse* series that weren't available in a store we returned to the library. We found books about sharks and books about dogs. These days we go to bookstores as often as we go to toy stores. We browse through the shelves of the children's section. We read back covers and first pages. My son devoured the Dinotopia series with an intensity formerly reserved for video games.

I knew he would love the Harry Potter books. He said no. His best friend loved them and lent one to him. No, he said. I read him the first chapter out loud one night. He said maybe. In child raising, when all else fails, my advice is: try money. I offered him a dollar a chapter to read the first book. The experts call this practice "hiring" a child. I call it bribery. It works. He began to read with a loud groan. After a few minutes I could see that shift in his attention that meant the book had him. He slumped at the table and then drifted down the hall with his face in the book and sprawled on his bed. Over the weekend he read all three Harry Potter books. I managed not to gloat.

This year my son read C. S. Lewis's *Narnia Chronicles* and Tolkien's *Lord of the Rings*. Still, it will be a while before he tackles Turgenev and Shakespeare. My daughter tried Jane Austen once: she read *Northanger Abbey*—and refuses to try again. That's okay. I've left a set of Jane Austen on our front table. I know the day will come when she will idly pick up *Pride and Prejudice* and read its addictive first sentence. "It is a truth universally acknowledged, that a single man in possession of a good fortune, must be in want of a wife." Whatever they read or don't read, my children are readers. They know the joy a book can give.

Since I learned to read, methods of teaching reading have been through two or three revolutions. There was phonics. There was whole word. Then there was chaos. There are flash cards and shapes. And there are even more theories about how to get children connected to books and literature. In my experience, learning is all about incentive, whether the subject is the capital of Nebraska as depicted on a plastic table mat or the symbolism of the rain in James Joyce's masterful short story "The Dead." In fact learning is also about content. The learning that goes on at our dinner table happens because my son is able to be the quizmaster, and as he hears the answers and checks them, he learns without knowing it. The learning that goes on when he reads a series of books, happens because he wants to know what's in the books and so he learns to read without even knowing that he's learning.

My daughter says she reads for escape when she's not doing schoolwork. Reading is the great escape. But as she's traveling in those imaginary realms of gold she's learning, learning everything from vocabulary words to human nature to the customs of another country in another time. Learning is much more than just learning to read or learning to recite poetry. Somehow, our children also have to learn to live, to get along in the world and to find a way to connect with friends and, eventually, with husbands, wives, and lovers.

How can we teach them these essential skills? This is where parenting stops and character begins. The answer is that we can't teach our children how to get along in the world, or how to stay married in the age of divorce. We can show them how to be responsible. We can be sure they grow up in a household where people aren't allowed to torture each other. We can try to pass on our own beliefs. Most of all we can listen to them. To be a good parent is to be a good listener. A good listener doesn't interrupt, not even to comfort. A good listener stays quiet until the speaker is finished. Then, after some deliberation, a good listener may or may not react. Usually a good listener's reaction includes some validation of what the speaker has said—after all, the speaker is taking the risk of confiding. But the good listener's reaction is almost beside the point. Most of us know what to do if we can only get a chance to hear ourselves talk about the problem. Children, more than adults, have an innate sense of justice and a reluctance to hurt other children. If we listen carefully, we can learn a lot.

. . .

LAST SUMMER in the playground near our house, I noticed a boy about my son's age on a gleaming new Schwinn bike riding shakily along one of the paths. A well-muscled young man in a stylish gym shirt jogged next to him, keeping up without straining, and murmuring friendly encouragement. At the end of the path, boy and man shared an exultant high-five, turned around and started back.

I noticed them because I have been teaching my son to ride a bike. Well, I have been *trying* to teach my son to ride a bike. I have bribed him; I have bribed his sister to teach him. I have spent hours jogging along behind him screaming helpful hints and breathless cheers. "Pedal!" I shout. "Pedal!" He turns at the sound of my voice and goes crashing to the pavement. It's not very stylish. There are few high-fives and some definite near-tears moments. I'm usually too out of breath to murmur friendly encouragement.

The kid on the Schwinn, I learned when I asked, is learning to ride a bike from a professional trainer. The professional does not yell. The professional is never out of breath. The kid feels great, even when he's still shaky. It's not just bike riding. More and more jobs which have always been done by parents are now done by professionals. My parents taught me how to ride a bike and how to swim. My father taught me to catch and throw a football with my fingers across the laces. This is now done by coaches.

My father taught me how to drive a car. I'll never forget being parked in the middle of a muddy, deserted field, the balky clutch on the old Fiat, and his sarcasm. Now most teenagers go to driver's education classes. Even something as personal as getting rid of children's head lice, which involves hours of nitpicking while the wriggly child sits still, can now be done by trained professionals. This outsourcing of parenthood has become so extreme that sometimes it seems as if actually giving birth is the only thing that can't be done by a better qualified professional—for a fee.

If I am critical of all this, it may be because I am jealous. It's obvious in one way that professionals, with their expertise and their absence of emotional baggage, can do a better job of teaching our children almost anything than we parents can ever do. They're professionals after all. I'm not immune. The memory of teaching my daughter to swim led me to enroll my son in swimming classes. They are both good swimmers. Only my daughter associates her first long swim with the sound of my yelling and threatening her.

I certainly would have been a safer driver, and a happier one, if I had learned the difference between neutral and reverse on an old stick shift from a driver's education teacher. Good tutoring is a wonderful way for children to learn. Sex education classes can be a less painful way to learn about sex than the embarrassed and embarrassing explanations of parents. Would I hire someone to wash out my child's hair and spend hours picking nits from each strand? I'd be tempted.

For most things, from learning to ride a bike to learning to read, my children have had to rely on me as I relied on my parents. They swim well, but they don't have the elegant strokes and speed of their peers who have been coached. Their schoolwork doesn't have the polish that tutoring can give. My son's handwriting is less than perfect; my daughter has trouble organizing her work.

But when I look back at my life, it's not my bike riding skills or even my college education that matter to me. What matters most in life—more than any skill or expertise—is our connection to other people. Life's greatest gift is the complicated, maddening, rewarding, and delicious involvement we have with those we dearly love.

The ability to be intimate with another person, even in difficult situations, is what seems to determine whether or not we lead happy and useful lives. That's what I hope I am giving my son out there on the playground as he skins his knees and injures his pride. That's what I hope I'm teaching my daughter when we disagree vehemently about the meaning of a novel. That's what I learned about, all those times when my father was fuming in the passenger seat. I miss my father. I am grateful that he was willing to spend those rainy afternoons with me so long ago. Although they aren't happy memories, I'd give a lot to have some of those moments over again. Those moments are worth a million hours of driver's education courses.

EVERYONE SAYS I should write about how you have to sit your children down and tell them all about sex. I've thought about this a lot. Of course children go through two different stages in asking about sex. The first stage, which happens at about age three, is when they want to know where babies come from. This is when you give them the famous sperm and egg talk. This is when you buy them those books and videos called *Where Do Babies Come From?* that make you squirm with embarrassment. This is the stage where all children ask at least one dreadfully embarrassing question in a public place. "Could I see your vagina?" your son asks at the supermarket checkout. "Where does he keep his sperm?" your daughter wants to know when an old boyfriend drops by for tea.

The more serious stuff happens when they are teenagers. Now parents are expected to explain what all of human experience has failed to explain. Why is sex so compelling? What is sex exactly? Parents are also expected to instruct their children in sexual and emotional safety. In fact, and remembering the dreadful moment when my father tried to explain sex to me, I have concluded that parents shouldn't tell their children about sex. Everyone I know has a horror story about their parents' fumbling, embarrassed efforts and their own mortification. In other countries, sex is taught matter-of-factly in the school system. There are plenty of terrific books on the subject. Let's give ourselves a break here. One of the most important things a parent can do is to keep lines of communication open. My children know that there is nothing they can't ask me; I hope they know that there is nothing they can't tell me.

THE ETHICS OF PARENTING

"YOU LET US MAKE OUR OWN CHOICES," my daughter says. "I think you trust that we'll know what's right for us. You let James choose what he wants to eat; for instance, he loves pasta and creamed spinach and that's not so bad."

Children need choices, but they also need limits. I try to make it look as if my children make their own choices. They think they are free and they are, sort of. Some aspects of raising children require direct guidance. Others require respecting our children's intelligence enough to explain the practical basis of right and wrong.

I remember the first time my daughter lied to me, more than five years ago. She was into witchcraft at the time, and one of the rules I had made was that she wasn't allowed to burn candles in the house when there was no adult around. She understood that this was a fire hazard. One day I walked into our apartment to find the place filled with the acrid smell of hot wax.

"You burned candles," I said.

"I didn't, Mom, I didn't."

"What's that smell?"

"It must be coming from the next apartment. I didn't, really Mom." She continued to protest as I walked into her room and picked up a candle, still warm, with liquid wax pooling at the top.

I didn't scold Liley. Instead I explained. "Listen to me," I said. "You must not lie to me. I don't have time to wonder if you are telling the truth. I don't have the energy to second-guess you. We have to trust each other or our family won't work." Because she understood why it was important to tell me the truth, because I shared the nuts and bolts with her instead of giving her a high-minded argument about the evils of lying, Liley became a truthful person. Later, she established a moral basis for truth, working it out for herself within her own belief system. Her honesty comes from her own heart. It's based on a decision I allowed her to make for herself, and it isn't imposed by my authority. If that hadn't worked, I would have tried another method.

More recently Liley stayed out with some friends at night, and forgot to call me when she said she would. Instead I got a call from another mother asking if I knew where the kids were. A few minutes later, Liley called, but those were terrible minutes. When we talked about this at length, and Liley had apologized, I was able to tell her what it felt like to get that call from the other mother. I was able to describe my anxiety. I told her that I didn't think anyone, under any circumstances, had the right to carelessly inflict that kind of anxiety on another person. I wouldn't do that to her, I said. I didn't expect her to do that to me. I didn't tell her what to do. I told her why she had to do it. It hasn't happened since.

The hardest kind of authority to use is the kind that doesn't appear to be authority at all. Yes, my kids pick the cards, as my daughter has noticed, but I stack the deck. I do let my children make their own choices, as she believes, it's just that I carefully choose the context of their choices. My kids can eat whatever they want, but I do the shopping. I try to buy what they like—within the boundaries of healthy food. Of course my children could do the shopping themselves, or they could demand special stuff every night. They don't, though. They do what most people do most of the time. They do what's easiest, and if I give them choices they are grateful, and if I make those choices pleasant they are absurdly grateful.

I like to say that I let my children watch unlimited television, and I do. The only hitch is that our one television is in my bedroom. To watch it comfortably you have to be sitting on my bed. This means that there are many times when the television is just unavailable. It's not unavailable because it's the television, it's unavailable because it's in my room. This also means that any show my children want to watch will probably also be watched by me, Mom. This means that they don't usually choose to watch television with friends and groups of friends. It's their choice, whether or not to watch, but they have to work around the limits of my bedroom. My children's access to the Internet is also controlled this way. My computer is the only one that has access, and it's in my bedroom.

I use the same method with my son and physical activity. My son hates to move. Given his druthers he would spend his life in one soft spot playing video games, drawing pictures, taking an occasional chess class, reading, and moving action figures around on the floor with a friend. Over the years, though, after much trial and error, I've discovered that he loves to swim. Sometimes he just bobs around in the water, but he loves the indoor pool at the end of our street.

When he asked to have swimming lessons, I obliged. When he wanted to stay after school to take a sports program with his best friends, I also fell into line. My son thinks he chooses to take swimming and do sports. Once in a while he decides not to. I say okay and he misses a few months. Right now he's swimming twice a week and spending an extra afternoon at the gym. It's his choice, but I arranged it so that making those choices was easy. Very easy.

When I want my children to do something—taking a sports class or taking a shower—I try to manipulate them into wanting to do it themselves. Sometimes I use the Br'er Rabbit method, named after the Uncle Remus story in which Br'er Rabbit begs Br'er Fox not to throw him in the briar patch, which is, of course, exactly what Br'er Rabbit *does* want Br'er Fox to do since the briar patch is Br'er Rabbit's home. Reverse psychology is best used in small doses, since my kids are extremely sensitive to the idea that they are being manipulated. What works best for me is to create a context in which any choice they make will be a good choice.

"I want you to have the illusion of freedom," I tell my daughter. "But I limit your choices, that's the trick." I tell her this because I don't keep secrets from my kids. People are just as easily educated if they know they are being educated, as when they are kept in the dark. When I explain my tactics to my daughter, she seems to like knowing that I spend this much time thinking about her welfare. The tactics continue to work. My kids don't really want equality. They want me to take responsibility for them. They are eager to be taught how to live. They crave rational authority. As I become a grown-up who has learned to wield authority in a loving way, my kids have become happy, stable, loving kids.

MY CHILDREN DIDN'T GET any of the things children are supposed to need in order to grow and thrive. Yet they are both healthy, successful children. What is it that my children got—besides their genetic inheritance, which is distinctly mixed—that worked so well? Looking back at our lives together, I see three assets my children had that may have contributed to their health and well-being. One thing I think they both have is the feeling of being useful. My daughter, who has borne the brunt of our chaotic life, knows that I couldn't do what I do without her. She understands that she's an important person in the family. Not only does taking care of her little brother enable me to work—and both my children understand that my work supports them—but she listens to my stories and makes suggestions, and she helps me with research and ideas.

When I was growing up, my parents had to manufacture chores for me so that they could give me an allowance. We all knew this was a sham. I was a kid who needed some responsibility—real responsibility—and perhaps that wasn't so unusual. Liley's bank account grows like an adult's because I often pay her for services that I would have to pay someone else for if she wasn't around. She's not just useful, she's indispensable. On the one hand her life is hard. She can't go to the Caribbean or skiing with friends even if she goes as a guest, because I need her at home. On the other hand, she knows that she's an important person in the world.

A second thing my children have is one omnipresent parent. I may be on the phone, I may be in a bad mood, I may be in my nightgown at lunchtime, but I am always there. Because I work at home these days, and because the only thing that's more fun than writing is not writing, I'm always happy to take them to school or pick them up. I'm one of the mothers who love to hang around the schoolyard. I'm the one who is arriving at school again an hour later because their child forgot something. My children may not have quality time with me, but they certainly have quantity time. I think that is tremendously important.

The third thing they got is a sense of reality. Their lives make sense. I don't have to think up chores for them to do to get their allowances. There are plenty of chores around our house that actually need to be done. If my son does his chores, I can do more work. As he bags the laundry, I am at the computer. He's around when I get the mail, and he sees the check that comes from the article I was writing. He's often there when I go to the bank. There is no mystery about how our family works. There is privacy in our family, but there are no secrets. Parents make mistakes, and children make mistakes. As long as those mistakes are made in a context of listening and fairness, in a world of cause and effect, and in a household where the parent is the responsible adult, they will be the kinds of mistakes that make us human, not the kinds that destroy our humanity.

PETS

ABOUT AN HOUR after I've tucked in my son, given him his last glass of water, and turned off his reading light—another light stays on in his room all night—I hear a thump. I don't want to hear the thump. These hours, the hours after my children are safely asleep in bed and the building and the whole neighborhood seem to settle down into quiet, are my favorite hours of the day. No matter how tired I am at bedtime, I seem to come alive when the last eye droops shut and the last cover is pulled up to the last adorable chin. Of course there's nothing to come alive for—I can't go out—but the combination of my sweet gratitude for my children and the sudden cessation of their needs gives me a burst of energy I would love to have at another time of day.

This is when I read, or answer my e-mail, or watch television, or do all three. Sometimes I call a friend in California, since it's usually too late to make calls in New York. So when I hear a thump, half an hour into this precious time of day, I try to pretend it's not happening. Then there's another thump. Then there's a thump and an odd scratching sound and a voice going, "Sssshhhh." I'm still in denial. Finally there's a thump, more scratching, and a burst of giggles. I put down my magazine and appear in the door of my son's room like a thundercloud. He's sitting up in bed, surrounded by white dog bones and mangled sheepskin dog toys. His new puppy is in his lap. "He couldn't sleep," my son says.

"He was lonely. He had insomnia so I was reading to him. You know, Mom, just the way you read to me."

Baby-sitters are invaluable help in bringing up children, and teachers also help a great deal, but much of the best help I've gotten has been from pets. Pets teach children responsibility, or at least that's what the experts say. In my experience they don't necessarily teach responsibility to the children, they teach it to the parents. But the family is a strange, passionate organism. Each family member plays a role, and each expresses both an individual self and also some part of the family dynamic. Pets help with this. They become a light, comic part of the family. They are like the leavening in bread. They love unconditionally. They don't take sides. They make everyone laugh.

I grew up in a household that revolved around our dogs, the dogs that made it possible for any of us to become useful adults. The air in our family seethed with feelings. Love was never simple, but wound around with criticism and fear. To love was to lose. The dogs didn't care. My mother, father, brothers, and I acted as if our dogs were really just furry, slightly stupid people. The dogs often wrote each other letters—they also wrote to their friends, the dogs of my parents' friends—carefully, hilariously misspelled and typed by my father. When I was away it was nice to hear from my parents, but a letter from my dog released a keen longing in me, and a sense of comfort at the same time. My parents were complicated. My dog was simple.

When my parents had something difficult to say to us children—whether it was criticism or information they thought we needed—they sometimes said it by altering their voices and pretending it was said by one of the dogs. "Where's Mom?" I might ask when she hadn't appeared at the dinner table. My father sat uncomfortably at the head of the table, leaning over the serving dishes. "She went upstairs," he would answer in a thin, nasal voice which I knew was meant to be the voice of the attentive dog sitting at his feet. "I think your father said something that upset her."

We usually bought dogs from people we knew well, or couples who had slid into breeding dogs when they got bored with the stock market or their advertising careers. All canine transactions involved quite a lot of drinking. Pet shop dogs were inferior dogs, we thought. The best dogs were "working" dogs like retrievers or shepherds—dogs which had been bred for some purpose other than pleasing their owners. Of course my father's attempts at training these dogs to do what they were bred to do were often hilarious. There were shelves of books on training and months of throwing dummies. Then my father would hire someone to take him shooting, finally succeed in bagging a hapless game bird, only to have his magnificent dog swim out to the bird, pick it up and spit it out. "Accchhh, feathers!" you could almost hear the poor dog complain.

At least our dogs weren't lapdogs, ornamental dogs. Lapdogs and dogs who wore sweaters were for other people. Our dogs may have been failures at actually retrieving, but they had important names which showed off the family erudition—names like Cassiopeia, Ezekiel, or Flora Macdonald, who was named after Bonnie Prince Charles's devoted supporter.

When I got married in the 1960s the first thing I did was to persuade my husband to acquire a dog. I didn't want to copy my parents. I found a breed which I felt expressed the softer, gentler life I planned to lead with my new family—a golden retriever. We named her Maisie. After a few years, we went to live in England. We left Maisie with my parents—they already had another golden retriever who had been adopted from my brother—and started shopping for British dogs. The English take their dogs very seriously. Through the medium of our desire to buy a dog we made many friends and spent many lovely nights in country houses visiting the families of puppies that we might want to buy. In the end we bought a pale yellow golden retriever from a championship family.

We drove out to Gloucestershire to get her and while she gamboled on the lawn the breeder served us a high tea on a two-tiered cart with scones and strawberry jam. We named her Bathsheba Everdene in the family tradition, and we called her Sheba. Almost immediately, little Sheba got a mysterious rash and we were plunged into a round of veterinary medicine that also gave us another way to look at the English. Sheba was fed a special diet of rice and chicken poached in its own broth which my husband and I were glad to share with her. When I asked if her dietary needs could be met in a store our vet drew himself up to his full height. "You wouldn't want to give her dog food," he said in an accent that made Noël Coward's sound like a drawl. "Absolutely not," I replied. I loved Sheba. It made my heart sing to hear her little barking noises. She was my faithful companion for many years, and she died a few months after Liley was born.

For a few years, after my father's death and my daughter's birth, our family had no dogs. It was a hard time. My love for my daughter carried all other loves before it. I thought a pet would just be superfluous. But ten years ago in the wake of my divorce from her father, my daughter and I spent months shopping for a puppy. We finally settled on Lydia. She became a family dog, a dog content to stay under my bed during the day and play with my daughter if asked. She is a calm dog. Her love is unconditional, but her aristocratic nature somehow seems to keep her from being demonstrative. If annoyed, she bites.

So when the time came for my son to have his own dog, I decided to do things differently. Getting a dog is something that happens slowly. First there are a few discussions which seem harmless enough, but the desire builds up a certain momentum. My son met a friend's miniature dachshund and was enchanted. My brother noticed a sign advertising a litter of miniature dachshunds in his veterinarian's office. I called the breeder and she had a puppy who would be available in a few weeks. Then she decided not to sell.

On a chilly autumn day I found myself in a pet shop—a pet shop!—writing a large check for a tiny six-week-old miniature dachshund—a dog who had won my son's heart by embracing him with his tiny paws and licking his face with a minute pink tongue. I suggested a few names: Rilke, or Goethe. After all, I explained to my son, dachshunds are German, so a great German writer's name would be appropriate for his new puppy. My son named his puppy Cutie. "Cutie!" I complained to the pet shop owner. "That's not even a name, it's an adjective!" No one seemed to care. By the time we left the store, the adjective was wearing a purple, shaker-knit turtleneck to protect him from the autumn chill. "He's shivering, Mom!" my son had protested when I balked at buying the sweater.

Word got out. My beloved brother—the owner of a Labrador named Miranda and a Portuguese water dog named Hannibal—laughed out loud when he heard what had happened. My mother—her Labrador is named Ida Tarbell—tried to be polite, but I could tell she felt sorry for me. Even my daughter and Lydia were a little haughty. My son was ecstatic.

CUTIE HAS BEEN LIVING WITH US for two years now. He ate the shaker knit sweater long ago. I've learned that he's a working dog after all, and I don't refer to all the hard work he does keeping my son up all night. Miniature dachshunds are bred for rabbit hunting. The dachshund chases the rabbit down the rabbit hole and grabs the rabbit in his tiny teeth. The hunter reaches in and pulls the dachshund out by his tail, and with it, the rabbit. And I have watched as Cutie, who tips the scales at a little more than ten pounds, has become a repository and a means of expression for the weight of our little family's hidden feelings—just as the big dogs with the fancy names were in the family where I grew up.

My daughter is an eighteen-year-old intellectual who makes a fetish of not caring about clothes. Appearances are beneath her notice. She is too serious to care. Cutie brings out another part of her. When she sees me playing with Cutie, she begins channeling his little voice— even as my father channeled Flora MacDonald's voice so long ago. "Oh Susan, is that spun cotton?" Liley lisps in her doggy falsetto as Cutie noses through my pockets looking for something edible. "Is that an Eileen Fisher sweater?" she goes on in Cutie's voice. "Susan, do you think you spend too much money on clothes? I don't think so, this is so soft." When my daughter doesn't like what I'm wearing she uses Cutie to express her opinion. "I don't think that pink is really you, Susan!" Cutie says speaking through Liley. When I offer my daughter advice on writing or about her homework, it's often Cutie who gently tells me to mind my own business. "Susan, I'm not about brains," he says in his "voice." "I'm all about looks!"

And Cutie helps my son let out his mischievous side. According to him Cutie is an adorable varmint, an irresistible bad, bad dog. "Cutie, have you been bad?" he asks and Cutie wags his entire body in de-lighted response. My son is a very good boy. He goes to bed on time. He brushes his teeth. He does his homework—that is, if Cutie lets him. "Cutie's keeping me awake," he'll explain when I find him reading after bedtime. Cutie always jumps up and wants to play when my son has

finished his macaroni and still has vegetables left on his plate. Cutie
steals my son's socks so that we are late leaving for school. Cutie is so
cute that my son can't concentrate on his homework. My son is never
in trouble—Cutie is always in trouble. He makes us all laugh at ourselves.

My true identification is with Lydia the corgi. Lydia is the older
dog, the distinguished dog, the dog who walks slowly, as if she had the
weight of the world on her shoulders. Like all dogs, Lydia expresses the
things I can't express. When we walk around the block together, I smile
at all my neighbors, even the ones I don't like. Lydia growls and barks
angrily. When I bought Lydia, I thought that I might move to a farm-
house in Vermont and breed Pembroke Welsh corgis, get rich, and stay
young forever. That's not how my life worked out. Lydia never got to
have children and now she has to deal with Cutie, a pet store dog. Lydia
and I have had some bad times and some good times. My life is filled
with wonderful gifts, so I don't let myself feel sad about times past. Instead I imagine that Lydia feels sad.

"You have to walk them, they're a lot of trouble," people say when
I suggest that children need pets. I want to ask what they were thinking
when they had children in the first place. Everything is a lot of trouble,
is the truth. If you ask me, anyone who, as an adult, is still worrying
about their own convenience is going to lead a very limited life. Just
like everyone else, I decided that our lives would be easier if Cutie was
better trained. Cutie needed to be housebroken, I thought. He needed
to learn not to bark unnecessarily. He needed to learn to sit and stay,
and not jump up on everything whenever he felt like it.

In the veterinarian's office I picked up yet another book on dog
training, a kind of New Age version of James Lamb Free's classic *Training Your Retriever*. Dogs don't obey people, because dogs think people
are dumb, the book explained. Dogs can run faster than people. Dogs'
sense of smell is sharper than people's. To train your dog you must show
him that you are superior, the book said. Human superiority to dogs is
based on their hands. Humans can throw, dogs can't. If you throw something at your dog, he will realize who's boss.

The next morning, when my son was at school, I decided to try
this. Cutie was locked in my son's room behind his gate, whining to get
out. "Cutie," I said in my most authoritative voice. "Cut it out. No

noise." Cutie gave me an appealing look as if to acknowledge my re-quest, and kept on whining. I reached into the room and held his mouth shut, catching his lips between his teeth as James Lamb Free rec-ommends. "No noise!" I said. Within a few minutes Cutie had resumed his whining, this time with a slightly accusatory tone. I reached for the water pistol, another highly recommended training device. "No noise!" I yelled. He kept whining. I let him have it.

Cutie looked reproachful, and water dripped from his silky little ears. He began to shiver. I went into my son's room, dried off Cutie and apologized. The minute I moved away, the whining continued. This time, motivated by the book I had read in the vet's office, I balled up two socks and threw hard. "I have hands!" I shouted at Cutie. "No noise!" The socks bounced off his head, and Cutie stopped whining just long enough to give me a look of absolute contempt. "Really, Susan," his expression said, as clearly as if he had a human voice. "Get a life!"

Teenagers:
Why We Hate Them.
Why They Hate Us.

You hear a lot of stories about people's teenagers. There are the bad teenagers who won't respect their curfew and stay out too late at night. There are the spoiled teenagers with their own cell phones and beepers and even their own sports cars. There are the disrespectful teenagers who are in trouble in school, the rude teenagers who won't get off the phone, and the delinquent teenagers whose parents are always having to bail them out of one sort of trouble or other. Teenagers! Parents of teenagers get together in support groups to share their stories of being disrespected and disobeyed. Dinner parties are taken over by tales of bad teens. Magazine editors commission stories about teenagers who drink too much, and teenagers who are sexually active. The news is dominated by teenagers who kill. Male teenagers are violent. Female teenagers are disruptive at best and pregnant at worst.

I have a teenage daughter. She is my close friend, and the most helpful and loving person in my life. She is a beautiful, graceful young woman who has respect for me in particular and for her elders in general. I'm not sure how this happened. I don't have a formula for producing wonderful teenagers. Perhaps I'm just lucky. I do, however, have some clues. I think a lot of the trouble we have with our children originates with our ambivalent feelings about their vibrant youth. I think our children make us angry at first, not because they behave badly, but because we are clinging to our own childhoods.

As a society we have romanticized childhood in a dozen ways. Children with their smooth skin and their narrow, unused bodies have become our ideal. Children's books top the best-seller list. Great children's literature is usually written by people who, in some way, remain children themselves. The vast majority of the great children's classics were written by British or American authors. I think it irritates us adults to be finally excluded from the golden years of childhood. We cling to them; oh how we cling to them!

Then when we have children of our own, we have to let go of the idea that we are still children ourselves. When they become young men and women, what does that leave for us? Are we to become old men and old women? It makes us angry that we have to grow old and die. It makes us furious that we are being relegated to a marginalized old age while our children take their places in the world we have loved so much. It feels as if we gave them everything; now they are telling us to move over.

Something has changed in the relationship of young men and women to their parents. It's not them; it's us. It's a hard, hard thing to watch a handsome, intelligent son or a dazzlingly beautiful, privileged daughter grow into their power as our own power diminishes. No one wants to let go of power. We may complain that we live in a youth culture, but perhaps we worship youth because it deserves our reverence. My daughter and her friends, the young students I teach, are an amazing generation of people. Whether it's the way their skin gleams, or the way their minds dance gracefully from idea to idea—I find them exciting and awe-inspiring.

When I walk down the street with my daughter, everyone looks . . . at her. I am invisible. I am in my fifties. Although I know better, when people we meet look into my daughter's huge blue eyes and want to help her, I bite my tongue. I want to say, "Hey! what about me! I'm paying for everything!" Recently an attractive friend my age complained angrily to me that all fashion was designed for young women. She had been to a fashion show with her beautiful daughter, and she had noticed that there were no cool clothes for women in their fifties. Of course fashion is designed for young women. Fashion photography is primarily restricted to images of young women. They look like angels! They look the way we want to look, even now, even when our time for looking that way is long since passed. And they don't just look wonderful, but they also have tremendous mental agility, extraordinary enthusiasm, and almost total recall.

It's a terrible struggle for us to grow up. Somehow being part of our generation meant signing on for eternal youth. Tune in, turn on, drop out—and now grow up? You've got to be kidding. Don't trust anyone over thirty has become don't trust anyone under twenty. Our life span may have increased, we may look younger than our parents did, but time is inexorable. We are getting closer to the end of this ride, the most wonderful ride, the ultimate ride. We can see the grim ticket taker up ahead at the gate. Our friends appear in the obituaries. We go to more funerals than weddings. Pictures of our friends' children and even their grandchildren show up in the wedding announcements. How can this have happened? And as we approach this sad ending, our own children, young and bursting with energy, are taking their seats with shrieks of exhilaration and anticipation.

Why are we so old and tired? It's because we have drained our hearts and our bank accounts to get our children the best seats on this wonderful ride. Straining forward toward the future, they don't even remember to look our way. Ungrateful! Disrespectful! After all, we don't want to be old. We try not to act old. We try very hard not to look old. "Old age is a shipwreck," William Butler Yeats helpfully explained. And because we are angry at our children, they are angry at us. Anger breeds anger. Hidden anger foments rebellion. Our teenagers' real sin is that they are inheriting our world.

THEN, AT THE END of the teenage years, parents are faced with the problems of college. First their child has to get into college. Then they have to somehow accept the turmoil, triumph, and sadness that goes with having a child leave home. When a child leaves for college it's a huge leap—no matter what the college. To make it worse, the press conspires to convince all parents and college-age children that it is practically impossible to get into college. For some reason the idea of exclusivity always excites the press. This is why we can all recite the *frightening* statistics: Only 10 percent of all applicants get into Yale. Harvard turned down sixty-five applicants with perfect SAT scores—perfect SAT scores! Tuition and room and board cost $36,000 a year at many universities. The *reassuring* statistics are harder to find: Seventy percent of all college applicants are admitted to their first-choice college. Few colleges expect anyone to pay tuition out of their pocket, and all colleges will work with parents to create a financial package.

My daughter is a better student than I ever was. Yet when the time came for her to apply to college, we were both caught up in a frenzy so intense and so time-consuming that it often seemed like a full-time job. Suddenly everyone in my daughter's class stopped talking about Dostoyevsky and biology and started talking about tutoring, scores, and college essays. Their parents seemed even more obsessed. At school, lectures on teenage alcoholism were replaced with lectures on college admissions. Instead of birthday parties, my daughter's friends gave early admissions parties. My daughter applied to eight colleges; many of her peers applied to fourteen.

How did this happen? In fact many of my most successful friends didn't go to famous colleges, and some of them didn't go to college at all. My father never went to college. There are no statistics to prove that going to a prestigious college has any correlation to the accomplishments we admire in the arts or even in business. Even a Harvard lawyer is often a lawyer who went to an obscure undergraduate institution before deciding on the law. So why are we pursuing a handful of colleges with an intensity usually reserved for a holier quest? Why are the college stickers on the back of the expensive cars in my neighborhood—the Swarthmores on the Volvos, the Yales on the Saabs, the Harvards on the Mercedeses—displayed with as much pride as the children themselves?

Perhaps it's because we think we own these beautiful sons and daughters of ours. Maybe we have mistaken parenting for proprietorship. If we do own them, of course we want them to have the best labels. A son at Harvard is to a son at the City College of New York as a Rolex Oyster is to a Timex—even if the Timex keeps better time. Even if City College has a better English department and our son wants to major in English. After all, our children are our most precious possessions and they are certainly our most expensive possessions. As an accessory, a child in an expensive school beats an Armani suit, a Kelly bag, or even the new BMW. This is why in status-conscious New York, the first question people ask each other is not, What do you do? But, Where does your child go to school? A new BMW is a nice car and a great status symbol; a BMW with a Harvard sticker on the back windshield is a nice car and an even greater status symbol.

My generation of parents is behaving as if we were applying to college all over again. We seem to have bought the idea—promoted by the colleges and by the press—that few things are more important than where a child goes to college. If we stop for a moment to think about it, we will realize that college actually happens one course at a time, one classroom at a time, one teacher at a time, one book at a time. What's good for one student may be poisonous for another. My goal for my children is that they succeed at love and at usefulness, and they may well learn how to do that at a college no one has ever heard of. They may even learn how to do that by embracing their own interests instead of going to college, as my father did. My daughter is fascinated by theology. Might she not do better as an intern at a seminary for a while instead of going to college? There is still a huge social component to American education. We all know that a good student could probably get through high school in two years, and college in two. My own daughter, when she took a semester off to go to school in France, did the academic work for the semester the summer before she left—in six weeks!

We all know that the kinds of pressure we are bringing to the college admissions process isn't good for our children. It isn't even about our children. At any rate, one of the principles of good parenting is teaching our children that childhood doesn't last forever. (Of course first we have to learn that ourselves.) Shouldn't we be teaching our children that life is rich with glorious opportunities, and that most of those opportunities happen after college is long passed? Ambition is important, that's true enough, but isn't acceptance even more important? After all, we have to live in an imperfect world. Maybe the college application process is a good place to begin learning that.

AVOIDING THE
BROCCOLI BATTLES

"Do you have any questions?" the pediatrician asked. I had nothing but questions. My two-day-old baby girl was lying, quietly for once, in my lap. My brain seethed with questions. "How can I keep her from having trouble with food?" I found myself asking. "How can I keep her from having a weight problem?" It was a big question. All my life I had been overweight or underweight, but no weight satisfied me. Food had always been my best friend and my worst enemy. I wanted to spare my beloved little girl this kind of torture.

"There's nothing you can do about that," the pediatrician said, with some impatience. He was thin. "It's all genetic." Perhaps our connection to food is genetic, perhaps each popcorn binge and skipped lunch is somehow encoded in our genes. But there are certainly things parents can do to help their children tend toward a healthy diet. Many books have been written about this. "I love my mom because she gives me food," my son has written on our kitchen cabinet.

We all know the basics of a healthy diet. Vegetables and fruit, grains and proteins, three meals a day, not too much sugar or fat. Getting children to adhere to a healthy diet is another matter entirely. The subject of food and children is one which excites passions and anger in parents. Clearly restrictions and force-feeding don't work. Generations of comedians have made fun of parents who force children to eat their spinach or their broccoli or even their Brussels sprouts. The awful truth is that no one can force anyone else to eat. I've used all kinds of leverage and threats, but I've discovered that my children will eat a fairly healthy mix of foods if they are left alone and if their requests are granted. My son loves creamed spinach, so instead of trying to make him eat broccoli, I buy him creamed spinach. Otherwise I try to offer many different kinds of foods, all of them healthy. And sometimes nothing else will do but a trip to Ben and Jerry's for a small cone of triple caramel chocolate fudge swirl.

WHEN SHE WAS SMALL, my daughter's eating seemed to provoke a dreadful anger in me. Meals together became terrible times. On one awful day I picked her up in Boston after she had spent a week with her father. I had missed her so terribly, my precious little girl. I couldn't wait to see her. She came bounding out of her father's car and pressed herself against me, and I felt whole again for the first time in days. I felt my heart heal up.

We went for lunch, and less than an hour later, in a restaurant on Newbury Street, I was hissing and clucking at her choice of food, at her dirty hands and her hungry, open-mouthed chewing. I was angry and critical, and quickly able to reduce the person I treasured the most—the person I had longed for every single minute that she was gone—to helpless tears. After that terrible day I tried to change, and eventually through therapy and prayer and enormous effort, I was able to change. I tried to unravel the anger I felt and the threads led back to my own childhood. I remembered how bad I felt when my parents criticized the way I ate. I reminded myself that, even though she was just seven, my daughter had a right to live her own life. I vowed not to pass on the legacy I had received in the house where I grew up—a legacy of using food as a battleground.

I swore to myself that I would never again mention my daughter's weight or try and control her eating habits. She could be fat or thin—that I could not control. What I could control was whether or not I used food to express anger. I could be sure that we didn't war over food. I was able to change. As time passed, I began to see my daughter as not being fat or thin, but as just being my daughter. I found her beautiful.

My love made her beautiful. I tried to offer her a choice of healthy foods, and otherwise I tried to stay out of her relationship with food. During years when she was overweight, I had the grace—and I know that this was God's grace—to see my daughter through the eyes of God. She was her beautiful self, never more, never less. If she didn't meet the standards society sets for young girls, I came to see that was irrelevant. After a while when people asked me how I felt about Liley's weight, I truly didn't know what they were talking about. My son is a big kid. Sometimes people—who knows what they are thinking—ask me what I am going to do about my son's eating problem. I smile at them and say, "Nothing."

This miraculous progression, from making a bad mistake, to realizing it is a mistake, to knowing how to act no matter how I felt, has happened over and over as my children have grown up. I know that if I think my children are brilliant and beautiful, my opinion increases their chances immeasurably. That is my first job as a parent, to love them unconditionally and accept them without anger. It's my job to believe in them. I know that my children are wonderful. I tell everyone. Adults have a way of rolling their eyes at each other, or making sympathetic grunts of complicity which are shorthand for complaints. Children know this. They hear. I never forget that my children are a gift and a blessing, and I think that's part of the reason why they are.

EATING DISORDERS

BY THE TIME I WAS A GROWN-UP, I had been on every diet that had ever been invented. I had tried Ayds reducing candy and I had tried mild amphetamines. I had gorged on eggs and meat with Dr. Stillman and baked hundreds of the cottage cheese and sour cream with sweetener concoctions known as Dr. Atkins Diet Revolution cheesecakes. I had eaten lentils and rice on Dean Ornish's and Robert Pritikin's diets and worked with a personal nutritionist who suggested that I write down everything I eat. I was a lifetime member of Weight Watchers, and a veteran of the Diet Center.

For a few years, when I was in my thirties, I discovered that if I ate only vegetables I could lose weight with thrilling rapidity. I couldn't get enough of losing weight. I couldn't get enough of buying clothes in single digit sizes. After about six months I stopped getting my period. I felt weak all the time. I still didn't feel thin. I visited a famous internist who told me that I should lose a few more pounds. He noticed that I had turned orange from eating so many carrots. He prescribed broccoli. I visited another internist who said I was suffering from nervous exhaustion. Eventually life intervened, and I, miraculously, got pregnant. This was the first way in which having a child saved my life—in this case literally. During my pregnancy I stopped dieting and ate my version of what the doctor suggested. I gained sixty-five pounds. After I had my daughter I went back on all the diets, and began losing weight again.

Then one afternoon in our kitchen, I watched as my baby daughter gorged on a plate of cookies while I loaded the dishwasher. Then she sucked her bottle so hard that her rosy little cheeks caved in. There was a hungriness in the way she ate that frightened me. I saw my own greed reflected in my baby daughter's eating, and I had a real epiphany. Our children mirror us, and in that moment I understood something new about my relationship to food. The problem wasn't weight, I saw, the problem was the way I ate. I began to read about eating disorders. I came to understand that I have a disease when it comes to food. I began to understand that people with eating disorders use food in exactly the same way that drunks use alcohol. Fat or thin, food seems to be the solution to all problems. In fact food is the problem. I learned that the symptoms of an eating disorder are not restricted to eating. They include self-loathing, obsession with food, a high from losing weight. I remembered that greed and gluttony are two of the Seven Deadly Sins. I found a name for what had happened when I lost so much weight that I felt weak and stopped menstruating—anorexia. I found a name for the throwing up my glamorous friends had done way back when we were in college—bulimia.

Just as I began to understand my own relationship to food, I began to see that my daughter's connection to food was also disordered. I'm not sure if she inherited this—I certainly come from a family riddled with eating disorders and alcoholism. I now understand some of the anger about food and eating with which I grew up. My daughter stands in front of a mirror pulling down her tiny sweater and pushing her rounded shoulders back at the air. She's a beautiful young woman with creamy skin, huge blue eyes, and a slender body. "Ugh," she says to her own reflection. "I'm so fat! I'll never eat again." A few minutes later she wants to know if I have any gum. A few minutes after that she's on her way out for Tasti-Delight, a low-calorie ice cream that tastes like frozen milk and is the hot cold food among East Side teenagers.

"You're not fat at all," I say. "You're beautiful. Have some gum. Do you need money? Is that your brother's sweatshirt?" I wonder at this. When my parents told me I was ugly, I believed them and I felt ugly.

When I tell my daughter she is beautiful, she doesn't believe me and she feels ugly.

"Unnh unhh," she says in self-disgust, although I've made her laugh, and in all situations that is always the right step. "I look gross! This shirt makes me look so fat!" I know, as surely as I know that she inherited my good legs, that she inherited this attitude from me.

A year ago, I threw away the scales. They had been on my bathroom floor for more than ten years—through three moves. Rust stains streaked their sides and the black surface was peeling away from the top. I treasured their consistency—I was always almost ten pounds lighter on my own scales than I was at the doctor's office. Each day, at least once, I went through the ritual of weighing myself. This ritual began at the bathroom door with a fervent prayer for thinness, and an exhortation to the God of diets to forget the M&M's which had somehow, through no fault of my own, before I was really thinking, found their way into my mouth while I was waiting to buy the tabloids at the newsstand on the afternoon of the day before. In the bathroom I took a deep breath, gripped the sink with both hands, and stepped on the scales. Then slowly I loosened my grip with my right hand, allowing my weight to descend on the scale, pound by pound. Then I let go slowly with my left hand. For one split second, I let go completely. Then I knew what to think of myself for the rest of the day.

The bathroom door was often closed during this ritual, but my daughter was watching me nevertheless. I was horrified by a scene she played out one Sunday morning when she was about three years old. I had left the newspaper on the floor while I was reading it. She toddled over and stepped carefully on a section of the paper with both little feet, and peered down at her toes in a perfect mimicry of my sacred weighing ritual. That scared me.

By the time my daughter was four, her pediatrician had decided she was overweight and should be tested by a specialist at Mount Sinai Hospital to see if she was at risk for diabetes. The doctor said that Liley was fine, but that she had a metabolism that was very efficient at manufacturing fat and holding on to fat. She was engineered to survive during a famine, the doctor said. She sent us to a food psychologist who spoke with us for a few hours and gave us three pads of stickers. He advised us to go home and put green stickers on healthy foods, red stickers on any candy we happened to have in the house, and yellow stickers on foods—like peanut butter—which were okay on a now and then basis. Now and then certainly does not describe my relation to peanut butter, and it didn't describe my daughter's either. I threw the stickers in the trash before we got home. Somehow I knew, even then, that food was highly enough charged in our household without putting little flags on it.

Although I successfully avoided having a war over food with either of my children, I have not been able to spare my daughter. It began in the sixth grade. Her homeroom teacher called me up to say that one of Liley's classmates and friends had come to her with some disturbing information. Liley was sometimes throwing up in the bathroom during school. When Liley came home, I sat her down and asked her about it. She wept with pain, guilt, and rage, and I tried to comfort her as best I could. She told me that when she felt disgustingly fat, or when she thought she had eaten too much, she found she could make herself feel better by throwing up.

That year was our family's *annus horribilis*. My husband had stopped drinking in January because he knew that was the only way to keep our family together. At first we had all been happy about being back together, but soon things began to go wrong. There were terrible fights. Nothing seemed to work. I know now that my husband was secretly drinking, and that this—even more than the drinking itself—was literally tearing our family apart from within. My daughter discovered that her stepfather was drinking. He lied to her. I believed him. I did a lot of traveling that year for work—disasters are always expensive—and Liley was left alone with her stepfather and her little brother. The whole thing just came down on her like an avalanche. She didn't know what else to do except vomit it back up.

I began reading everything I could find about bulimia. I went back into therapy. I looked for help. I found an eating disorder specialist who dealt with teenagers and I sent my daughter in for a consultation. Eventually I changed her pediatrician to a doctor who is an expert on teenage girls. Now when she's feeling shaky, she has the resources to help herself. Slowly our family got better.

Still, the morning after I threw away the scales was a bad morning. At about six o'clock in the morning I heard a shriek from the bathroom. "Mom, where are the scales!"

"I didn't know you were weighing yourself at dawn," I said, groggy with sleep. I explained my good news. I had thrown away the scales. I wasn't going to be enslaved by a silly, inaccurate number. My daughter didn't think this was good news at all. She was outraged. I suggested that she should be happy. I invited her to join me in freeing herself from the bondage of the number on the scale, a number which had never been accurate anyway.

"I know. That's why I needed it!" she exclaimed. But she was laughing.

In the months since, I have been accused of ruining my daughter's life, and wanting her to feel fat. I have been called a traitor for weighing myself at the gym. Recently I started weighing myself at a local drugstore. One morning the proprietor suggested that I would weigh less if I bought something. "We have a button right here," he said. "The more you spend, the less you weigh." I bought five bottles of shampoo; my weight did not change. My daughter laughed so hard when I told her about it that it was worth every penny I had spent. I haven't lost my self-righteousness, though. I no longer creep into the bathroom and lower my body down on an ancient contraption invented for the torture of twentieth-century women. I suggest that if my daughter wants to punish herself I won't stop her. She can buy a scale herself, along with some fat calipers and one of those machines that goes "oink" every time anyone opens the refrigerator door.

Recently, new scientific studies have shown what has been fairly obvious to anyone who noticed—that eating disorders have a genetic basis. Like alcoholism, eating disorders are family diseases. They destroy not only the person whose eating is out of control, but they harm everyone around them. The distraction, irritation, and self-hatred engendered by an eating disorder can throw a whole family permanently out of balance.

Alcoholics often say that eating disorders are small potatoes compared to alcoholism. No one ever was arrested for "fat driving" they joke. I beg to differ. As a police reporter I saw more than one accident caused by women who—on their way home from the supermarket—

were so distracted by unwrapping the food they couldn't wait to eat that they drove off the road. Anyone who is thinking about food the way an addict thinks about food is not listening or watching much else.

As American life spans lengthen and health and appearance standards grow more stringent, our national eating disorders are thrown into sharp relief. As smart as we are as a nation, we still expect people's eating patterns to make sense. Of course they don't. We are mystified by the fact that, as more and more emphasis is placed on health and eating patterns, our obesity rate has soared. Shouldn't it be the other way around?

This is what it means. In many families, food is used as a drug to anesthetize feelings, and as a means of self-expression to show love or anger. As any addict can tell you—whether they are addicted to heroin, or Equal, alcohol or popcorn—anxiety about addiction strengthens the addiction. We use food to calm our anxieties and to reward ourselves. When we don't want to feel, we eat. We teach our children to do the same. In order to avoid worrying about obesity, we eat.

I HAVE LEFT MY CHILDREN alone together for the first time for a weekend. I am interviewing someone in California. A friend stayed with them the first night. Our neighbors have been alerted. My daughter is eighteen and my son is ten, but although I might well have hired an eighteen-year-old to take care of my ten-year-old, this is different. They are two kids left alone together. Last night my son had a fever, and this morning my daughter tells me how frightened she was. It's so scary, she says. I woke up every hour to check on him. It is scary. God knows it's scary. Children are so precious and so fragile. I know she's all right when she makes a joke. "Note to self," she says. "Be sure to have children who immediately grow to be ten years old." We both laugh. I go back to work.

CHILDREN AND ALCOHOL

FOR A SCHOOL PROJECT a few years ago, my daughter decided to do a survey of our neighborhood stores. She wanted to find out how hard it was for a fourteen-year-old kid to buy beer. She was a young-looking fourteen-year-old, and I assured her that her quest was useless. She would be carded, I carefully explained. If she didn't have proof of age, she wouldn't be able to buy liquor. I had seen other teenagers get turned away at local markets. I had even seen markets refusing to sell cigarettes to high school kids. No one would be blind enough or stupid enough to sell to a fourteen-year-old child. It was illegal. Within an hour she was home with three six-packs and a couple of wine coolers.

At three supermarkets in our neighborhood she had bought beer without even being questioned. Only at our local market was she stopped. She explained that she was buying the beer for her father. The owners of the market have known my family for five years, and they have never seen any sign of Liley's father. They happily accepted her excuse. I don't even know why I was surprised. Many of the advertisements in the news magazines that my daughter reads for pleasure or for school are for liquor, and many of the people in the ads appear to be teenagers. Television shows we watch as a family—sports and game shows—are punctuated with liquor ads featuring cute little animals and sitcom situations. A classmate of Liley's did an art project based on

Absolut ads, and liquor is the drug of choice for many New York teenagers. It's legal—more or less—it's easy to get, and it's socially acceptable.

We live in a culture that doesn't take alcohol very seriously—so how can we expect our kids to take it seriously? Compared to the way we feel about drugs or even cigarettes, alcohol gets a skip. It shouldn't. Almost half of all fatal car accidents are alcohol-related, and many of those accidents involve teenagers. A quarter of all hospital admissions are alcohol-related. Domestic violence, burglary, and rape are all tied to alcohol and drug abuse. Almost every violent story in the news conceals the use of drugs or alcohol by one or more of the participants. Alcohol is toxic for the body and the mind. Yet many teenagers are allowed to drink what they want, paid for by their parents, as long as they don't get into serious trouble with their school or with the police. That's a very low standard. What we have in our society when it comes to children and alcoholism is Absolut blindness.

I grew up in a world where drinking was one of the principal privileges of adulthood. The rattle of ice and the good feelings which preceded my parents' cocktail hour was as sure an indicator of the coming of evening as the darkening of the sky. My father would pour an Irish for my mother and then his own whiskey without ice. Neat, he called it. My parents were always in an excellent frame of mind around dinnertime, and they were often very cranky in the morning. I began drinking seriously in college, and drank most of my life. I felt that having wine with dinner, or stingers afterward, or sherry on Sunday was a human right, up there with the right of free speech and the right to bear arms. After all, the Puritans had more liquor than water on the *Mayflower,* didn't they?

All this alcoholic cheer finally turned ugly, as it always does. It took a long, long time for me to learn the terrible price of those soaring moments when I felt that I could walk among the stars. These days I don't drink. My kids don't see me drink; they don't see me drunk. There's no liquor in my house. I don't think this is the bottom line, and I understand that many people can drink safely. Still, if I don't want my children to drink, I know that the single most powerful and effective tool I have is my own behavior. If you do something—whether it's drinking, lying, cheating, or charity and service—your kids will probably do it too. Parents may think that, because they are adults, they can handle the risks involved in drinking, smoking a little pot, or taking mood-elevating pills. That's not how it looks to kids. Children don't listen to their parents—they watch them.

There's also no question that the tendency to become addicted to drugs and alcohol is passed from generation to generation, and that makes it a special kind of parenting problem. If there is alcoholism or drug abuse in your family, your children are at risk no matter what you do. The question is how to handle and minimize this risk. One way to help is to provide children with as much information as they can absorb. There are lots of excellent books about drug abuse and alcoholism. If you give your children those books they will pile up on a desk and collect dust. If you read those books and educate yourself, you can find ways to impart the information to your children. Before they decide to drink, teenagers should know what alcohol is doing to their young bodies, and they should also know what it may do to their lives. Kids think they are invincible. Information about what can happen, combined with parental concern, can help to make them careful anyway. There are no tried-and-true answers. There is no real protection from alcoholism.

There is one other thing we can do for our teenagers which will protect them from drinking too much, as well as from all the other dangers inherent in being a young man or woman in this world. We can pay attention to them. We can listen to them. We can create families where alcohol and drug abuse are taken seriously. We can teach them. We can make sure that we keep the lines of communication open. We can be sure they know that we will never stop loving them—no matter what they do. That's a parent's real job.

Listening is one of the most important tools of parenting. I spend more time listening to my eighteen-year-old talk than I ever did looking after her when she was an infant. As an infant, she needed me twenty-four hours a day for her basic physical needs. I remember the years where I couldn't take a shower without enlisting someone else to watch her for those few minutes. Now her needs are even more important, and almost as time-consuming. She needs the psychological equivalent of that full-time nurturing she had as an infant. If anything, she needs me even more than she did then, as a sounding board, as a confidant, and as a friend.

As an infant, her needs were simple. A baby-sitter could meet most of them if I wasn't around. As a teenager, her needs are complicated, and although friends and teachers can help her with them, she needs me in a more personal and intense way than she ever has before. Now she is making the decisions which will shape her life, and many of those decisions are about friendships, interests, and how to handle temptations. My daughter tells me almost everything, but she often tells me everything only after hours and hours of telling me almost nothing.

Time itself is infinitely malleable—but rarely in the way we want it to be. In moments of ecstacy time speeds up. In moments of boredom it slows to a crawl. Think about time spent in a traffic jam. The minutes go by like hours. Then think about that golden moment which was your last successful vacation. Because time has a mind of its own, I try to be sure that I spend as much as possible with my children. Hours pass in companionable silence as we go about our business. I write a column while my son plays a video game or does his homework. I make a salad while my daughter chats on the phone. I talk on the phone while my son tries to teach his puppy to sit. I clean up after the puppy while my son bags the laundry. Sometimes we borrow a car and just drive around. Mostly we do nothing. This is quantity time, listening time, time when nothing has to happen.

The most extraordinary times we have—times of joy, times of deep connection, or times of frightening honesty—only come after hours and hours of ordinary time. Any researcher can tell you that the last ten minutes of a two-hour focus group are when the important things are said. As an interviewer I often notice that in the last few minutes of a long interview, in the time when I have turned off the tape recorder and put away my notebook, a subject often says the most important things he or she has to say—and often in the most eloquent way. It's the same with kids.

If you ask my son how he is feeling, he'll tell you about his most recent triumph in a video game. If you take him swimming some afternoon, hang around the cafeteria while he perfects the art of making and shooting spitballs through a straw, and join him for a snack, as you amble home he might surprise you by revealing that he's been on detention for a week at school. If you don't react to that information with anger, or criticism, he might even tell you why he's been on detention. If you keep on listening, he could even let it all out, the whole story, what happened and the way it felt to him.

If you ask my daughter how she's doing, she'll say "fine." If you sit around chatting with her about her friends and her teachers, and if you listen carefully to her account of how Mindy said the wrong thing in history honors and Miss Crumb was mean to her about it, and you keep on listening while she says how worried she is about her friend who is getting thinner and thinner while no one seems to notice, she just might tell you that she's decided to become a vegetarian but that lately she's been feeling tired all the time. In this case, as in many cases, it's my job to provide her with information. I can buy her a book about what vegetarians need to do to get enough protein, or I can send her to the Internet. It's not my job to judge what she is doing. It's my job to help her do it intelligently. It's only by unrestricted listening that I find out what her problems are at all.

Even when I can't listen, I try to be there. The principal of my son's school has the gift of being everywhere, and it's one of the things that make her a great educator. It's a big school, with five floors and five hundred children in six grades. Somehow, whenever you look up, there is Shelley. I don't know how she does it, but I know that it has a tremendous effect on the spirit of the school. I try to do that as a parent. Whatever happens, I want my children to feel as if I'll always be there, whenever they look up, whenever they need me.

I try to give my children independence, but at the same time I know where they are at all times. As a child, I often left our house late at night and got into all kinds of potential trouble. Morning found me very hard to wake up in time for school. I make sure that my children are in bed at night, I check on them when I wake up. I leave my bedroom door open, and I leave theirs open too unless they object. Most of all I stay very, very involved with my children's lives. I never snoop in my daughter's room. I don't have to. I'm in there all the time, delivering her laundry or looking for something which has mysteriously disappeared from my room and magically reappeared on her desk. I'm often in my son's room too, looking for a toy he has lost or building new shelves for his latest creations. My children are children. They need my protection. I try not to confuse letting go with looking away.

In the family where I grew up there were lots of secrets. Secrets can destroy a family. Alcoholism was one of our big family secrets and it hid in the most difficult place to find—it hid in plain sight. No one dreamed that my parents or anyone they knew were alcoholic. Drinking was just what adults did, the same way they ate or breathed or wore clothes. Other family secrets were not spoken about. There are many good reasons for keeping secrets from children. Each parent has to decide, on a day-to-day, minute-to-minute basis, how much of the real world their child can manage—in every area from the playground to the private lives of their parents. I believe that adultery should be kept secret from children, for instance. As an adult, though, when my parents' secrets began to have repercussions on my own life, I was better off knowing what was going on. Children shouldn't be burdened with the alarms and conflicts of adult life.

But how can children understand their own experience if it's not based on reality? If a parent is sick or depressed, or if there are acute financial problems, these will affect everyone in the family. If children don't know the truth, they will make up their own truths. They will slowly lose touch with reality as they spin desperate fantasies which try to make sense of what they see and feel. Usually these fantasies feature bad children, unloved children, children at fault. Almost invariably these fantasies are far more damaging than the truth could ever be. They will become crazy with a kind of insanity reserved for those who can't get the information they need to navigate the circumstances of their lives.

HOW LOVE WORKS

AND I WONDER, what have I taught my children about love? They stand at the threshold of life, with all of life and love, marriage and sexuality spread out before them. I wonder what they will make of it. Will they be able to succeed at giving and receiving the kind of love that we call "love" as successfully as they give and receive the love of their family and friends? All I can hope is that they don't follow my example.

My relationships with men have been disasters. There have been long disasters—some lasting as long as fifteen years—and short disasters, but they have all ended badly. I try to have a sense of humor about this. Still, I am often aware and sometimes sad that in this one area I have failed, and that my failures have caused a lot of pain to other people as well as to myself. My ideal, the ideal of a lover who is also a friend, has eluded me. Whether I am the pursuer or the pursued, the one who loves the more or the one who loves the less, whether the man is a citizen or an outlaw, someone I have just met or someone I have been in love with for a decade, the outcome seems predetermined by my own attitudes and behavior.

My connections to men and the insanity that surrounds those connections have done a great deal to harm my children. I left my daughter's father and then linked up with my son's father. When my son was three years old, I left my son's father. When I have been involved with men, I have had less time for my children. One lover convinced me that it was better for my children to model adult love. They should see that two people could love each other, he said. That was more important for them than having me around all the time. They would understand by watching us that adult love was possible.

Looking back I can see that many of my connections to men have been shadowy replays of my connections to my parents. There is always pain. There is always betrayal. There is always tremendous, surprising dishonesty. This is my song, so to speak, the timeless unconscious playing out of my innermost images and characters on the stage of my life. I can only hope that my children will have different images. Or that, whatever currents their unconscious sends them as guidance will not overwhelm their reason.

When I ask a friend who has three wonderful adult children what she thinks is the most important thing a parent can do for children, she says, "Be predictable." It's an answer I've heard before, and of course it's a right answer. Children who know what to expect from their parents have an easier time in life. Parents who are punctual, reliable, and constant provide their children with a security net. They know how the world works.

There is another way to think about predictability. It is important for parents to be reliable, but the nature of life is to be unpredictable. It's a great gift to be reliable for your children, but you must also teach them to deal with unreliability. Nowhere is this clearer than it is when it comes to love. Love is unpredictable, and in love our own feelings become supremely unreliable. The love of a young man or woman—their desire to be close to the one they love—can change to disgust or indifference from hour to hour.

"You're sending me mixed messages," my daughter complained one evening when I had urged her to go out with friends soon after giving her a short lecture on family responsibility.

"It's my job to give you mixed messages," I said. "You should go out with your friends. You should be responsible to your family. Opposites can be true."

But parents who are themselves unreliable and unpredictable provoke a terrible yearning in their children. When a parent promises one thing and then does another, a kind of feverish hope springs up in the terrible gap between the fantasy and the reality. When that happens again and again, the child begins to dream that someday, someday if they behave, someday if they wish hard enough, someday the parent will do what was promised. Their love becomes hungry. That hunger, that desire to merge fantasy and reality, is compelling and painful and creates a longing to see and be with—and change—the beloved parent. That yearning gets mistaken for love.

When we are waiting for someone, when a child is waiting for a parent, tension builds. Soon the child begins to want the parent to show up—and wanting that becomes a longing to see their dear face. All anger—where are they anyway?—is forgotten and subsumed in this desire to see them. The more the child waits, the more anxious the child becomes. Love and anxiety are forever intertwined. My son's relationship with his father is like this. My relationship with my son's father was like this. Of course, my relationship with my own father was like this. My son's father takes pride in being unreliable. He argues that lateness is a virtue because punctuality is a vice. His lateness is legendary. Sometimes he is days or even weeks late for an important event—my son's birthday for instance. He was two hours late for our wedding ceremony.

A friend of mine with grown sons tells me that she is watching them make the same mistakes she made. I pray that my children will not have to do this. I pray that having one boringly reliable parent will remove the glamour of a parent who is always just about to arrive. I also know that we live in a world where confusion about love is built into the fabric of our society. Love, the feeling they write the songs about, is not a reliable feeling. That's what makes the songs so sad.

I talk with my children as if love were a rational thing. I tell them that having children is the best thing that ever happened to me. I apologize to them for all the suffering that my crazy heart has caused them. I tell them that I love their fathers. It took a while, and years of therapy and years of prayer, but I love both the men who are the fathers of my children. I see them as struggling human beings just like all of us. I wouldn't want to live with them, but I don't have to. I hope that will teach my children something about love. Mostly I hope that whatever happens in their hearts, they can stay calm. Love is a great wrecker of peace of mind. If I can teach my children to value themselves, and if I can help them to treasure their own peace of mind, I think they'll go out into the world with some chance of avoiding my many, many mistakes.

When the three of us have dinner together, my son says grace. We sit around the table, or in the living room with our plates in our laps, and we give thanks. "Lord, make us an instrument of thy peace," my son says, in a short version of St. Francis's ancient prayer, and my daughter and I join him. Sometimes we hold hands. "Where there is hatred I may sow love," we say. "Where there is injury, pardon; despair, hope; sadness, joy; darkness, light." Then my son grins and looks pointedly down at the two dogs already sitting alertly under the table in case any scrap drops to the floor. "May we have peace both top and bottom," he says. That's what my father used to say at the end of grace at our family meals. And when we start eating I am overwhelmed with gratitude for my beautiful children, for their health and their humor and for all the wonderful things in our lives—including peace both top and bottom.

Believe

BY THE TIME MY DAUGHTER WAS BORN, eighteen years ago, I had stopped going to church on Sunday. I was wary of organized religion. Any casual student of history knows all about the atrocities committed in God's name and the dreadful wars fought over ridiculous liturgical intricacies. Righteousness scares me, and holy righteousness scares me even more. Still, the birth of my daughter was a miracle, so I went looking for the God who might have been responsible for such a miracle. It was Lent, the forty days before Easter, and I visited dozens of churches, dropping in for the mass, or a prayer, a few bars of organ music or a portion of a sermon. In my own New York way, I was shopping for God.

On Easter morning of 1983, I happened to find myself at early communion in an Episcopal church on Fifth Avenue. At first the service seemed predictable enough. The language of Thomas Cranmer's Book of Common Prayer sounded as majestic as a wonderful poem by Yeats or Shakespeare. As the minister began his homily, my eyes were caught by a flash of color at the end of my pew. It was a bright green egg, hidden behind the prayer cushion. Then I noticed a lavender egg next to the hymnal. There was a yellow one on the floor at the communion rail and another one in the corner of the door to the sacristy. I knew that I had found my church.

Getting my children to church was a trickier proposition. Of course I wanted us to be one of those storybook churchgoing families—Mom in a broad-brimmed hat, sister in a smocked dress, and brother in a pint-sized navy blue blazer. I knew that parental righteousness is as scary as any other kind of righteousness. Why don't you come to church with me? I would ask my daughter. It gave me great joy to see her at the communion rail receiving a blessing—after all, she was the reason I went to church in the first place. After she turned six, though, she decided not to go anymore.

I was never forced to go to church, but I used to go with my father. After the service he would take me out for breakfast. Stacks of pancakes with maple syrup were definitely worth kneeling in a damp pew for half an hour while a minister droned through the prayers for the people, and I dutifully recited the Apostles' Creed.

As an adult my search for God has been much more complicated. For one thing, I have had to stop looking for meaning and start looking for faith. I have come to believe in a power I call God; my life has been the scene of miracles, beginning with my children. I have also come to believe that God is beyond my understanding. That's why my searches for meaning are meaningless.

Faith is not something I will ever have, the way I have the keys in my pocket. Faith is my ambition; it's what I aim for on good days and struggle toward on bad days. I needed that faith when my daughter decided she was a witch, and I need it now that she's going to college. I find God in strange places sometimes—in the voice of a friend, in an afternoon walk around a Revolutionary War battlefield, in the golden light of summer afternoons. Usually though, I feel God's presence when I am with other people who form some kind of community with me, and church is such a community. Something happens at the communion rail that I can't even begin to describe in words. It's as if my heart is momentarily in sync with a mysterious harmony. The same thing happens sometimes when I look in on my sleeping children, or when I see a friend I love glowing with health, or sometimes just for no reason at all. God is beyond reason.

MY SON LIKES TO WISH ON THE EVENING STAR. Although we live in New York City, I have shown him how the first star in the sky appears just at twilight, as the dark drops down over the East River and the buildings where we live next to a park. That's the wishing star, I tell him, as my father told me a long time ago. "Star light, star bright, first star I've seen tonight. I wish I may, I wish I might, get the wish I wish tonight," I have taught him. My father always told me that he wished for a gold watch and chain. I always wished to be beautiful. When my son asks if he will get his wish, I have told him that I don't know. But my son's wishes are tremendously specific and intense.

My son does not wish for new crayons or less homework. He wishes for his father's presence. He wishes that his father would miraculously come around the corner walking his dog and say "Hey, boo" to my son as if nothing could be more natural. He wishes that the lights of airplanes across the river landing at LaGuardia Airport, which sometimes look like stars, were the lights of a plane from California bringing his father.

When I realized what my son was wishing for, I suggested to him that—along with wishing—he might want to pray. I told him that if there was something that he really wanted, he could pray to God for that thing.

"Then will I get what I wish for?" His voice held the excitement of a promise, of a way to manipulate the universe in his favor. Here at last—this God business—was the answer, the wish that would always come true, the path to freedom from pain.

"I don't know if you will get what you pray for," I told him. "All I know is that if you pray, your prayer will be heard." What I don't tell him is that I have come to see that I don't know what is best for me. I have often been denied what I have prayed for, and I have often been glad I was denied.

I believe that God, or whatever name we want to give God, lurks in the interstices of our lives. Raising my children has taught me a lot about God. When I notice the perfect synchronization of my children's need for independence with my ability to let them go, when I contemplate the amazing and improbable biological nature of childbirth, I can see that there is another force in the universe, and that force is benevolent. I begin by calling that force my God. That force suffused my life with the birth of my daughter, and that force has been my secret

weapon, my best friend, and my surest adviser as I have raised my children into being the amazing, thrilling creatures they have become.

In life, all pain comes from attachment. I have friends who have
acted on this revelation by trying to keep themselves from being too attached to anything. Parents don't have that liberty. We are already attached, hopelessly attached, attached beyond all reason. Yet within that
attachment, within my passionate love for my children, I have managed
to cultivate a sort of detachment which comes from my belief that
there is another force in the universe besides human force, and that
force is benevolent.

It's hard to believe in God in our secular world. God is really the
last taboo, but without God, without the belief that some other force is
helping, raising children is infinitely painful, frustrating, and miserable
for all concerned. I believe that each of my children has a separate path,
a separate God. I don't necessarily know what's right for them, and I
definitely cannot protect them.

I was visiting a friend once when my daughter was about two—a
time when I could hardly bear to let her out of my sight. She was the
most precious thing in the world; I only felt at peace when she was in
my arms. I watched in amazement as my friends' teenage daughter got
dressed to go out. A group of local kids pulled up to the house in a
pickup truck and honked. My friend's daughter bounded out of the
house. My friend waved at the boy who was driving and walked out to
say goodbye. She seemed to mean it when she said she hoped they
would have fun at the concert they were going to in a nearby city. She
didn't even stand in the road and watch as the truck with her daughter
in it drove out of sight. I was flabbergasted, and clutched my own
daughter closer. My friend didn't seem to be thinking about accidents,
drugs, sex, and all the other bad things that might happen to a young
girl in the big world. "How did you do that?" I asked her. She laughed.
Later she told me that in order to raise her children she had to believe
in God. What other choice did she have?

Almost every story I can imagine is packed into the Book of Gen-
esis in the Old Testament, and the story of how we must raise our children is no exception. When I first read it—the story of Abraham and
Isaac—I was horrified. Abraham loved Isaac dearly. The little boy was

an unexpected gift to a couple who thought they were too old to have children. In the story, God told Abraham that he must kill his own beloved boy and burn him as an offering to the Lord. Forget it! That was my reaction. Abraham, however, obediently prepared to do as the Lord commanded. He took Isaac with him, packed a knife for killing the boy, and headed for the place where the Lord had told him to make the offering.

There is a moment in the story filled with a parent's anguish. It comes when the innocent boy Isaac asks how they can make a burnt offering if they have brought no lamb to offer. Abraham does not tell his son what has happened; he does not treat his son as a pal. He keeps his fear and heartbreak to himself, knowing—as good parents must know—that it's an adult's job to protect a child from certain truths, at the same time telling them what they need to know for their own understanding. Abraham tells his son that the Lord will provide. In its blunt, powerful prose the story lets us imagine how Abraham felt as he tied up his beloved son and prepared to kill him. At that moment, of course, a lamb appears and the Lord tells Abraham to untie Isaac.

This is a cruel story, but it echoes the extreme feelings parents have about their children. In fact this cruelty, the importance of giving our children up to situations that feel dangerous, is what the world inflicts on parents every day. When I send my beautiful daughter to school every morning, I do so in full awareness of how easily a taxi could jump the curb, a brick could fall from a building, a random object thrown by someone could zero in on her. When I send my son off to go bowling with a friend, I imagine with intense vividness the hazards of the subway system, and his willingness to talk with strangers. It feels as if I am being asked to make an offering of them. I am only able to let them go because I believe that the world is a benevolent place—that there is a God. I don't understand God, but I don't have to understand God to trust God.

For the first years of my daughter's life when my friends asked me when she was going to school, I replied—seriously—that she wouldn't be going to school. I just couldn't imagine my cherished baby being out of my sight for the length of a nursery school day. The world is a dangerous place, I explained to my friends. Of course she did go to school, nursery and then kindergarten and now she's going to college.

It's evidence of the benevolent harmony of the universe that as she was ready to go out in the world on her own, I was ready to let her go. In eighteen years that have passed like a moment, I have gone from being a mother who couldn't let my daughter out of my sight, to being a mother who is proud that my daughter is living by herself in a dormitory.

I remember my own parents' distress when I first asserted my independence. I wanted to walk around the block by myself. I was five. They let me go, but years later my father told me that he had shadowed me, hiding in doorways and behind parked cars to avoid making me feel that I couldn't do it on my own. By the time we moved to the suburbs when I was eight, I was allowed to wander at will in the woods and fields around our house, and even along the suburban streets where my friends lived with their families. Perhaps the world was safer then, but I'm not sure of that. There were hundreds of accidents that might have befallen a careless kid on a bike—we didn't wear helmets in those days—or a kid fascinated—as we all were—by the drama of the railroad tracks which separated our neighborhood from the Hudson River.

At what age is it all right to leave a child alone for an hour? How old must a child be to walk the dog by herself? To get to school on his own? To travel by herself after dark? These are some of the most difficult questions parents face, and the right answers vary. Recently our local newspaper took a survey of dozens of parents to find out how much independence they give their children. I read the survey avidly looking for some kind of guidelines. They weren't there. My son is ten. Some of his friends walk back and forth to school by themselves, some even take the public bus. Others aren't allowed to leave the school building until their parents or baby-sitters have arrived. By the time they are twelve, most of them will be navigating the city streets on their own.

There has been a slow, harmonious letting go that has happened with both my children—and that seems to happen unnoticed with most children and their parents. I didn't do it. One of the many miracles involved with raising children is that our instincts seem to be eerily synchronized with our children's needs. Some natural harmony is at work here, which lessens our attachment to our children at the exact speed at which they need to become independent. When Liley was an infant, she needed me most of the time. She needed me to feed and clothe her. It felt right to be with her all the time. It was literally inconceivable to me that I might not see her for a day or two. Now that she is eighteen, she needs to go out and maneuver through the world on her own, with her own faith whatever that may be. That feels right too.

No one is equipped for parenthood. No one can imagine what it's like to have an infant. Even after infancy, even after you can return to the sanity created by being able to sleep—more or less—six or seven hours uninterrupted, parenting is still the ultimate impossible job. Realizing this, admitting this, admitting that I need all the help I can get from my family, my friends, and God, has helped me a lot. Most jobs have a beginning, a middle, and an end. Not parenting. In most jobs there are successes and failures. Not in parenting. Often children who fail in school are extremely successful in life—even in the most conventional ways. Often children who do well in school fail miserably in life. There are no job reviews for parents. There are no measurements for parenting.

There have been many bad moments in my life as a parent. There have been many times when I have felt completely unqualified to be anyone's parent. This feeling rolls over me like a thick fog. Sometimes it happens when both children urgently need me at the same time. My daughter is talking on the telephone with her father. She hangs up and bursts into tears at the same moment that my son slams the window on his finger in another room and starts to cry loudly in pain. I feel helpless and incompetent. By now I know that feelings of helplessness and incompetence are a useless self-indulgence. They are another way of saying, hey, what about me? When I say that I had to stop being a child myself in order to be a good parent, that's one of the things I mean. I had my chance to be a baby. Now I am a parent.

This is harder than it sounds. When my son's father is away, my son grieves. I want to say to him, "What about me? What about everything I do for you?" But I don't. In the elevator on the way to a birthday party I look over at my son. My son looks sad and there are gray circles in the smooth skin under his eyes. I reach over and kiss him lightly on the cheek. With one dirty hand he reaches up and rubs the place my lips have touched, as if to rub away the kiss. This is the boy whom I have loved, fed, provided for, comforted, schemed for, plotted for, cheered for, and love. On this day alone I have taken him to the zoo with one friend, bought and wrapped a birthday present for another friend, and now I am taking him to a party. He rubs away my kiss? He misses his father? It would be easy to tell him how I feel, but I remember that I am the adult.

When we reach our floor, my son's friend leaps out to surprise him. Big smiles. My sulky son chatters away and hands the friend the present I have wrapped. I remember that I love my son, and that my love requires nothing in return. That's what they call unconditional love. Unconditional love is based on nothing—no conditions, no tests, no standards, no kisses. It's unconditional love that children need to grow and prosper. Only an adult can give unconditional love. An adult who is still a child will be thinking: What about me? What about my needs?

I have been a parent for almost twenty years now, and I wonder what I have learned. I have found a way to believe in God and that helps me allow my children to lead their own lives. I have learned to get along on very little sleep. Most of all I have learned to love. To say that having a baby changes your life is a great, great understatement. Having a baby explodes your life and you may or may not be able to find your old self among the pieces. I remember the girl I was before I was a mother. I thought that if only I had this or if only I had that I would be happy. I look back at that silly young girl with compassion—I think of her almost the way I would think of a daughter.

ON WEEKDAY MORNINGS my daughter likes to wake up before dawn to study. She sets her alarm for three. I go into her room when I kiss her good night and reset it for four or five. I try to make her go to bed at nine. I've told her, at least a thousand times, that she needs eight hours of sleep. It's obvious that she doesn't, but she's too nice to point that out. Someone once told me that when I found myself saying something over and over, or even more than once, I should stop and ask why I was repeating myself. If a child doesn't respond to something the first time, that child isn't likely to respond the seven hundredth time either. The complaint has to be rephrased, or the situation changed somehow. I still tell my daughter to pick up her room; she still lives as if she were in a dormitory. At least I know that the problem is with the command, not with the child.

Her dressing usually wakes me up. We live in a long narrow apartment, and anyone moving around in it is enough to bring me to consciousness. I have friends whose children sneak out at night; as a child I snuck out at night. I'm happy to have a living arrangement that makes me aware of who's coming and going. I go back to sleep to the sounds of my daughter making her breakfast and leashing the dogs. Waking my son is completely different. One of the reasons I am thrilled to have two children is that they are so individual, so contrasting in every way. Having two children allows me to see which parts of their behavior come from being children—all children have tantrums at a certain age, all teens get teary—and which are theirs only, their gifts of character. Their differences also remind me of my own powerlessness. Although I believe very profoundly that parents alter children's lives, I also know that children are very much themselves from the moment of birth—possibly from long before that.

I've never used ice or cold water to get my son out of bed, but I may have to soon. My daughter hates to sleep in the morning; my son hates to sleep at night. On weekends he'll sleep until noon if nothing disturbs him. I try to make his first waking moments pleasant with a kiss or a greeting. Usually within a few minutes I'm pulling off the covers and raising my voice. I'm thinking, Two decades as a parent and I still haven't got this one right. By the time he's up my daughter is gone. She likes to get to school when the doors open.

My son hates school even when he likes school. Although my son is my size, I lay out his clothes and give him five-minute warnings. I pack his lunch. The walk to school is one of the sweetest times of my day. It's a pretty four-block walk, and we're both relieved to have made it into the street with our clothes on. We are always late. My son complains about school. I explain to him that we often have to do things we don't like in this life. We pass the same people every morning. We all smile shyly at each other, like newcomers at a dance.

THIS AFTERNOON I walked my son home from school in the golden light. It's spring and the trees are blooming with their lacy white blos-

soms and drooping with their heavy pink blossoms and the block asso-
ciations have planted the earth around the trees with daffodils. It's my
daughter's eighteenth birthday and we stop to get her a present at the
neighborhood toy store. We try to decide between a stuffed pig—my
daughter's favorite movie is *Babe*—and earrings. I'm for the earrings;
my son favors the pig. "She has enough stuffed animals!" I protest. He
gives me a look of loving contempt. We get the pig. It will sit on her
shelf with her menagerie, next to the special place for Real Me.

At night both my children are asleep, and I peer into their rooms
and check on them in their beds. My daughter is sideways on a pillow
with her astrology blanket neatly pulled up, and a huge history text-
book face down at the edge of the bed. Next to the pillow are her favorite animals. Real Me and Reptor, the green dragon who went to
France with her three years ago because Real Me was too fragile. Her
long dark hair fans out against the covers and gleams in the low light. I
wait there until I can hear her breathing, and imagine her sleeping in a
golden net, a net of grace and protection.

My son has tossed off the covers. He's lying, surrounded by shelves
of books, Lego creations, and toys, on his bed with both his arms spread
wide toward the ceiling. His table is piled with Pokémon card wrappers
and video game boxes anchored by Nintendo controllers. The book he
was reading as he fell asleep has fallen to the floor and shut. *Dealing with
Dragons,* a book he has read and reread. In his sleep he giggles at something in a dream and then rolls over toward the wall. His puppy is curled
up beside him with only a little nose poking out from under the crum-
pled quilt. The room smells like chocolate milk. In the distance I can
hear the sounds of the city at night, horns and a siren far, far away down
by the river. I stand there looking out at the buildings across the way
and the few stars I can see, and I say a prayer of gratitude. There is a
sweetness to my sleeping children that is almost a smell, that I can almost feel in the air, and that swells my heart as I stand there, just on this
one night when he is ten and she is eighteen and I am lucky enough to
be their mother.

EPILOGUE

A BOOK ABOUT CHILDREN can be finished, as this one is, but the children are never finished: they continue to grow and change, to delight and challenge. They fill the heart and subvert the minds of their parents. Raising children remains an impossible job. There are no experts. There are no hard and fast rules. Nothing works; everything works. I have tried to describe the deep connection between parent and child, and to suggest that the parent has as much to do with what happens as the child. There are no bad children—only bad situations compounded by bad attitudes. In my own experience of rearing two children, I have seen that the principal problems parents have with their children stem from a desire to be children themselves. This book is about authority, the abdication of that authority, the abuse of that authority, and—I hope—a description of a workable balance between the two.

Since I finished this book, my daughter has gone off to college—she's a freshman at Princeton—so now I fall asleep with one child under my roof. Liley's departure has been pretty smooth—seeing her triumphantly take up her own life makes me so happy that it more than outweighs any sadness I might feel. My eleven-year-old son sorely misses his older sister, but he also thrives as an only child. A couple of times this fall, he and I have just rented a car and gone down to spend the day with her on campus.

Last year, the principal of my son's school left to work at the district level. Next year, my son has to change schools, so we spend a great deal of time visiting schools, reading about schools, and preparing to take tests and give interviews. This process of finding a school he likes seems to have expanded into being a process of finding out more about who he is. He's a boy who lives to stay home and putter, so a school far away is not likely to be worth spending two hours on a bus. He loves mathematics and science. He loves his friends and wants to go to school where he'll find at least one familiar face.

As I write this though, it's Thanksgiving weekend, and I have been falling asleep listening to both my children's breathing again as I did for so many years. I peek in on Liley, still hugging a stuffed animal, still asleep in the bed where she has slept for most of her life, and then on James, curled up next to the puppy who is now almost three years old, and I know what Thanksgiving is all about.

ACKNOWLEDGMENTS

IT TOOK AT LEAST A DOZEN VILLAGES to write this book about raising my children, and hundreds of helpful villagers. There's the village where I live and where my son goes to school—our neighborhood in the east eighties. My children were my most valued assistants, serving as subjects and editors. At their request I rewrote many sections, leaving some anecdotes out and including others. To protect them I have used their middle names, Liley and James. I also changed some other names.

There's the village of Simon & Schuster, where Sydny Miner's belief in this book made it possible and where the brilliance of Michael Korda and Chuck Adams made it perfect. There are the villages of my children's schools, the Manhattan New School and the Convent of the Sacred Heart, whose educators and teachers helped me raise my children and collaborated with me on their educations. There's the village of *Newsday,* where editors Phyllis Singer and Ginger Rothe helped me write a column about raising my children, which taught me more than it could possibly have taught my readers. There's the Bennington College Writing Seminars Village, where I took my children twice a year, and where they saw people actually living lives devoted to poetry and to studying writing, and where they learned to sled. There's the village of Yaddo in Saratoga Springs, the one place on earth where being a writer feels normal. There's Witherspoon Associates, where President

Kim's incisiveness discovered my passion for this book in the flotsam and jetsam of an afternoon's conversation. And there is *Architectural Digest,* where Paige Rense taught me most of what I know about class.

I like to think of books as cooperative efforts. Without my friends and my neighbors, my brothers and sisters-in-law, Ben and Janet, and Fred and Mary, my mother, my family, without the incomparable Stanley Arkin, without the hundreds of people who talk to me—from the other mothers in the schoolyard to the people who write me letters—I would be lost. You wrote this book, all of you who have lived and raised children along with me. All of you who have struggled with the passions and contradictions of parenting, all of you who have helped me or been helped along the way. Thank you.